MW01119742

SOCIOLOGICAL SOCIAL WORK

This book is dedicated to Brad
Priscilla Dunk-West

Dedicated to Pauline Verity
Fiona Verity

Sociological Social Work

PRISCILLA DUNK-WEST
The University of South Australia, Australia

FIONA VERITY
Flinders University, Australia

ASHGATE

Published by
Ashgate Publishing Limited
Wey Court East
Union Road
Farnham
Surrey, GU9 7PT
England

Ashgate Publishing Company
110 Cherry Street
Suite 3-1
Burlington, VT 05401-3818
USA

www.ashgate.com

British Library Cataloguing in Publication Data
A catalogue record for this book is available from the British Library

The Library of Congress has cataloged the printed edition as follows:
Dunk-West, Priscilla.
 Sociological social work / by Priscilla Dunk-West and Fiona Verity.
     pages cm
 Includes bibliographical references and index.
  ISBN 978-1-4094-4507-4 (hardback) -- ISBN 978-1-4094-4508-1 (ebook) --
  ISBN 978-1-4724-0108-3 (epub) 1. Sociology. 2. Social service. 3. Social service--Practice.
I. Verity, Fiona. II. Title.

 HV40.D824 2014
 361.3--dc23

2013029930

ISBN 9781409445074 (hbk)
ISBN 9781409445081 (ebk – PDF)
ISBN 9781472401083 (ebk – ePUB)

Printed in the United Kingdom by Henry Ling Limited, at the Dorset Press, Dorchester, DT1 1HD

Contents

List of Figures and Tables

Figure

Table

Notes on the Authors

Priscilla Dunk-West is a sociologist and registered social worker. Her scholarship is concerned with identity/selfhood, professional selfhood and self-making. She researches in the area of selfhood, sexuality and gender and professional self-constitution. Over the past 13 years she has divided her time between Australia and England where she has worked both in social work practice and in academia. She is currently senior lecturer in social work and academic head of field education at The University of South Australia. In 2011 she co-edited, along with Trish Hafford-Letchfield, *Sexuality and Sexual Identities in Social Work: Research and Reflections from Women in the Field*, published by Ashgate. Her latest book *How to be a Social Worker: A Critical Guide for Students* uses an interactionist notion of self to understand professional self-making in social work.

Fiona Verity is adjunct Professor of Social Work, Flinders University, South Australia and both a social worker and sociologist. Before academic life she worked for 17 years in community development and management roles, mainly in the community health sector. She has maintained an active engagement in working with community organisations. She has conducted research on the impacts of insurance and risk management on civil society after the collapse of the insurance company HIH, food affordability and access, and community based health promotion. Her recent post was Dean, School of Social and Policy Studies, Flinders University. With Joy Noble, she is the author of a little book called *Imagine If: A Handbook for Activists*, published by Wakefield Press.

Foreword

There are many pioneers whose work sits at the interface between social work and sociology and yet there is a paucity of this tradition in literature. Although researchers and educators in social work may adopt a sociological position in understanding social work areas of practice and ways, there are few words in social work lexicon which can be used to describe this. If practitioners are using sociology in their practice, as we did in our respective practice, there was and is a lack of a named theoretical tradition to describe this. *Sociological Social Work* is our contribution towards introducing a type of practice and orientation to the world which is evidenced through theory and research. In this book we make the case that there is no better time to adopt a sociological 'kaleidoscope' in viewing and understanding the world within which we live and work. In this way, *Sociological Social Work* is as much for researchers and social work educators as it is for practitioners and students.

If there is a positive from the technical/rational (Lupton 1997) world of the professional, it is that it pushes social workers to be clearer about their theoretical orientation and the type of research they draw upon in framing their practice. Our hope is that in response to the question: 'what theory underpins your practice?', the answer is 'I was using a sociological social work approach'. Our hope is that there is a return to the prominence of the 'social' in 'social work' and that sociological social work opens up a rich new world to researchers, practitioners, students and academics alike.

We write as social workers who have practiced in advanced industrialised contexts – Australia and the United Kingdom – where social work is part of the tradition of both the welfare state and the non-government sector, and where there have been significant debates, and often quite rehearsed, about social work's purpose and ideological underpinnings. We write as social workers committed to social justice, which affects the ways in which we make sense of the world and what we hope for social work. Our narratives are derived from our own experience in research, practice and teaching and yet we are mindful that these representations speak to particular types of social work. We argue that it is important to understand individuals and society through thinking about the interplay of social units and the global. We hope that *Sociological Social Work* will be seen as the continuation of a conversation that has been present since the origins of social work: one that can continue and alter, shift and respond to our new world and its related challenges, including interpreting past practices, as well as imagining into the future.

Priscilla Dunk-West and Fiona Verity
May 2013

Acknowledgements

This book was developed over a number of years and we are grateful to Claire Jarvis from Ashgate, both for her initial enthusiasm as well as her continued dedication to this project. We have had institutional support from each of our academic institutions, both Flinders University and The University of South Australia, in the writing of this book. We acknowledge the support of Georgia Allan for her editing work.

Table 4.1 from the Productivity Commission 2010, *Contribution of the Not-for-Profit Sector*, Research Report, Canberra © Commonwealth of Australia, Productivity Commission is reproduced by permission.

There is much to be said for the occupation of the space between disciplines: this book is as much a contribution to this terrain as it is a bridge between sociology and social work. We acknowledge the historical legacy of the connections between sociological theory and social work practice and the development of the contextualisation of the individual within their social and interpersonal contexts. We hope that our small contribution to such a perspective offers new potential for the building of research, theory and practice and a more clearly articulated sociological social work. We have been thankful that in this project we have been, to boldly quote Isaac Newton, 'standing on the shoulders of giants' of those who have developed sociology in social work.

List of Abbreviations

AASW	Australian Association of Social Workers
CBT	Cognitive Behavioural Therapy
GEC	Global Economic Crisis
HCPC	Health and Care Professions Council
IASSW	International Association of Schools of Social Work
IFSW	International Federation of Social Workers
NFP	Not For Profit
NGO	Non Governmental Organisation
SCIE	Social Care Institute for Excellence

Chapter 1
What is this Book About?

Introduction

Social work is deeply optimistic and in the concern for social justice and empowerment is an intellectual and emotional commitment to better worlds, human wellbeing and equitable material and social relations. In the context of rapid social change and digital technological developments we contend that thinking sociologically is helpful as an ever present reference for making sense of the social work purpose and how this is realised in spite of challenges emerging in a transforming world. It enables insight into the historical and institutional processes which have got us to where we are now, and how we take these insights into future practice. It does, however, require solid intellectual groundings to equip social workers well for the work they will do.

The focus of this book is the constitution of social work concepts, approaches and practices fit for new times: both the times that are new to us and for times that are new because of the order of social change. The way we approach this is through exploring and expounding upon sociological social work. Sociological social work is a kind of social work which is animated by a life-long sociological interpretative perspective. It is practiced by social workers able to engage their sociological sensibilities and requires knowledge about social work and sociological theories about the world and our day-to-day interactions, both with the people with whom we work and the agency/public policy context. This chapter is an elaboration of the aims of the book and the relevance to social work education and practice. It focuses on theoretical interpretations of contemporary social dynamics and change and empirical data about our shifting world. We will conclude this section by providing a brief description of each chapter, legitimising why the chapters are integral to social work theory for work in a changing world.

Social Work and Times of Change

Each and every day social workers in their practice encounter a diversity of subjective experiences that are kaleidoscopic fragments of bigger, dynamic and changing stories of agency and social structures in a transforming world. Social workers support individuals, families and communities by understanding impact and consequences of poverty, unemployment and injustices, abuse, conflict and violence, housing shortages and illness. Social workers will work directly with individuals/families and groups when they need assistance, undertake prevention and development work about individual and collective concerns, and engage in applied research and policy advocacy. In certain situations social workers engage with people on an involuntary basis because of state requirements, and in other contexts they work with non-government or voluntary agencies. Because of the varying institutional bases of practice there are countless ways social work will take place.

Despite this variation a constant aspect of the social work mission and this applies irrespective of the social work approach taken or the specific agency mandate, is that the issues that people and groups live with cannot be split from the wider context of historically shaped social, economic and political relations and practices (Ife 1997). The International Federation of Social Work definition of social work is as follows:

> The social work profession promotes social change, problem solving in human relationships and the empowerment and liberation of people to enhance well-being. Utilising theories of human behaviour and social systems, social work intervenes at the points where people interact with their environments. Principles of human rights and social justice are fundamental to social work. (http://ifsw.org/policies/definition-of-social-work/)

'Empowerment', 'liberation', understanding the interactions of people within their environments; these aspirations make it an imperative that the social worker sees the bigger picture in their work. One aspect of the bigger picture is attention to the organisational context wherein social workers are employed; the policy agendas, program directives, criteria for service use and regulations of practice. It too means thinking about social work practice in the context of public policy making and the broader public policy frameworks that impact on social contracts and resources for social work practice. It means reflexively knowing that the experiences that face the people and groups with whom social workers work are shaped within the hegemonic or normative discourses, practices and expectations within the society. It also means knowing about the 'environments' in which people live their lives which is a 'dynamic, changing system' (Ife 1997, p. 26).

Thinking about these bigger picture questions requires what C. Wright Mills (1959) called a sociological imagination, as dually a 'craft' and a 'promise'. This imagination is a quality of mind to see, in a historical context, the links between the micro and the macro, or the ways in which private pains (like ill-health, or unemployment) speak to public troubles (Mills 1959) (caused by pollution or structural weakness in an economy which means workers lose their employment). One of the attributes of this imagination is the capacity to situate human experiences in the times and relate the now to human history, both in respect to the past and the future.

Whilst each generation and each era is a change and continuation from the one before, there is a body of literature that distinguishes our current time, the period around the new millennium, as an especially transformative period of social change (Beck 2000; Lemert 2007). Castells goes so far as to call this a 'new world':

> ...at the end of the twentieth century we are living through one of those rare intervals in history. An interval characterised by the transformation of our "material culture" by the works of a new technological paradigm organised around information technologies. (Castells 1996 p. 29)

This does not deny that new worlds have happened before, as of course they have. For example, the European plague in the mid-1300s is estimated to have killed almost 25 million people: this is a tragedy easily distinguishable as heralding a new order. What are now called developed nations radically changed in the eighteenth and nineteenth centuries as a result of the advances in science and technology associated with industrialisation, bringing with those changes a radical shift in previously defined roles around work and family, leisure and mobility and with consequences for power relations and experiences of oppression and freedom (Giddens 1991). Industrialisation processes now underway in China, India, Indonesia and other developing countries are changing social and economic relations within these countries, and at a pace.

A feature of *our* new global world, that is, our contemporary world, is attributable to the unprecedented rise in new digital technological communications and both the hybrid and homogenous forms of globalisation including global capitalism, with the institutional embedding of neo-liberal values. These developments have radically changed the ways in which we live our lives (Giddens 1991; Urry 2000; Beck and Beck-Gernsheim 2001; 2005). New technologies for example have enabled everyday activities to speed up, or in the words of Lemert '...we are beginning to see that the world is becoming what it is becoming because of speed' (Lemert 2007, p. 165–6).

The world which preceded email communication, for example, communicated differently: things took more time. Prior to emails, there were office memorandums, hand written or typed, faxed or duplicated by hand. In contrast, there is now instantaneous communication so long as each party has access to the right technology. The moment an email is sent, it is received by the sender regardless of geographical bounds. Alongside these new conditions, new expectations for instant replies bring with them new occupational stressors, expectations and roles. Another example is the photograph. Whereas the digital camera produces its snapshot instantaneously, in previous years photographs required development: removing the film from the camera and taking it to a shop for processing took time. Processing film was the dominant way that images were captured as little as one generation ago. If you yourself do not recall previous ways of doing things, the chances are your parent will recall a life pre-mobile telephones, pre-internet and pre-email. The ways in which we interact have changed markedly due to these technologies. For some, this makes the world a smaller place, whereas for others continued inequalities take new shape in digital divides and exclusion (Castells 1996).

However new digital technologies also open up possibilities and spaces to do different things and do things differently. Never have so many people moved around the world as they do now, even without leaving their homes. The number of hits on Youtube and political blogs outside of political parties illustrates levels of participation on matters that concern people and the global reach and impact of this communication. Some sociologists theorise that this contemporary order of social change is distinctive. Not only are the developments in technology enabling new forms of relating to others through new identities, the ways in which we live our lives are being shaped by developments relating to the pursuit of work and leisure. There is clear evidence that in 'making' through the use of technologies we are, in fact, being creative and 'connecting' with others (Gauntlett 2007; 2011). It is just that it looks different to the ways in which we have connected with one another in the past.

Alongside the uptake of new technologies and forms of relating, there is some evidence that the demarcations between work and private life have become less compartmentalised (du Gay 1993; Dunk-West 2011). This order of change evokes parallels to earlier times of change when both social work and sociology were born. Kickbusch situates change in alignment with key historical developments:

> The shift from the industrial societies of the nineteenth and twentieth centuries to the knowledge societies of the twenty-first century is as groundbreaking as was the shift from the agrarian to the industrial world, and the diseases that come with this change are of a larger societal, not an individual nature...New forms of working and communicating are shaping our working life and lead, for example to new issues of worklife balance. (2008, p. 9)

Kickbusch further argues that we 'need new policy mechanisms' and a 'shift to a new mindset for health and society' (Kickbusch 2008). She suggests the uptake of 'prevention labs' as incubators for new understandings and practices. Specifically this means the creation of spaces where people can think and deliberate about the world as it was, as it is and as it is changing. Martinelli (2003) poses the question about the usefulness of the concepts we use in social analysis, and whether they are up to the task of making sense of this world. In the spirit of such engagement, the question that runs through all of this book is how best to engage in sociological social work that is fit for the emerging issues and challenges of the twenty-first century. In other words: how do we engage as sociologically thinking social workers in the context of change? How do we read our society, the multiple environments that shape clients' lives and the ways in which it and they are changing?

The premise of this book is that these changes have implications for how social workers think and respond to the issues they face in practice from a place of discernment, and in ways that do not bifurcate 'micro and macro', and reduce highly complicated social relations and interpersonal dynamics to only matters of what individuals know, think and do. Furthermore how do social workers reconcile what they learn in university courses about social justice values and practices and what they may be required to do in practice, in organisations steeped in neo-liberal values? How can social workers influence the systems in which they operate? What is their responsibility in bringing about change for the better in relation to such systems? What might guide such work? The contemporary social work practice environment with all of the inherent contradictions heightens the challenge for social workers to maintain critical interpretation, avoid enculturation and stay clear about social work purpose.

We argue in this book that there is no better time for social workers to have sociological thinking abilities to see and understand the changing world, and act with social work purpose, than the present. Sociological social work, we argue, ought to be used as a way to name and justify a kind of practice in which sociological theory comes together with social work aims. Sociological social work is also a sensibility: it marks a particular orientation which helps in addressing some of the key challenges which emerge in our changing world. There is potential arising in the new world for the realisation of social work's purpose: how do we interpret these and take positive action? Indeed how do social workers notice and name the changing conditions which are so easily eclipsed in the busyness of practice? This is a quasi-new project, for the relevance of the times to practice is a basic question in social work; experiences, meanings and the actions and impacts in practice are inseparable to a broader social, economic and political context. Not only is the world and social change speeding up, but theoretical debates are moving in leaps and bounds; new work emerges on agency and identity, mobility and mobile lives, cultural forms, risk and trust, family and social change.

Our perspective builds on an established critical tradition in social work. This tradition can be traced back to social work's roots and has been the preoccupying focus of practice for many social workers in practice. There have been some key thinkers for whom a sociological lens has been primary and their work has been influential; for instance the works of Dominelli (1997), Ife (1997), Mullaly (1997), Schwartz (1974) and Leonard (1966).

This book elevates and names the importance of such an approach which we argue is critically needed if social work is to achieve its agenda in transformative social, political, economic and environmental contexts. Social theories are consistently applied to practice settings (Ferguson 2009; 2011; Garrett 2012; 2013) yet these are often framed as existing 'alongside' or 'with' or 'for' social work. We argue throughout this book that sociological social work is one answer to the question: what theory or theories underpin your practice?

In this chapter we outline the material we discuss, sociological social work. The scope of this book extends to all fields of social work practice. It will encourage a way of thinking and political and social awareness which, we argue, supports social work practice in the shifting landscape that it is placed within. The text will not deal exclusively with particular areas of practice but the examples used are drawn from a range of social work settings including an international appreciation of social work.

Our concern in this book is to take these rich sociological ideas which can remain abstract and can be selectivity read and draw connections with them and the practical work of social work. This is more than 'borrowing' particular traditions or scholarly ideas and insights from social theorists. Following the lead by Domenilli we suggest that sociological social work is invaluable for active engagement with this knowledge thereby adding to the body of social work knowledge. We follow contours of time, self, identity and agency, community and solidarity, bureaucracy, the capitalist market and climate change to bring these ideas to life.

Before moving on to examine some of the key ideas related to this task, it is important to explore definitions which help to convey the meaning of both sociology and social work and situate them in their historical contexts.

Sociology and Social Work: Born in the Same Cradle

Sociology is a discipline, an endeavour, and a sensibility. Giddens describes sociology as:

> ...the study of human social life, groups and societies. It is a dazzling and compelling enterprise, as its subject matter is our own behaviour as social beings. The scope of sociological study is extremely wide, ranging for the analysis of passing encounters between individual in the street to the investigation of global social processes. (Giddens 2005, p. 2)

Here Giddens highlights the two broad areas of interest in sociology: the individual, and broader society. There are a number of theorists associated with sociology, as we shall see throughout this book. As Giddens points out, sociology is concerned with things which we encounter in our everyday existence, and this can make it difficult to analyse, since it is so familiar (Garfinkel 1984). Bourdieu points out that this is primarily a challenge to the way that we think. He says:

The difficulty, in sociology, is to manage to think in a completely astonished and disconcerted way about things you thought you had always understood. (Bourdieu 1991, p. 207)

Bauman and May (1990, p. 5) strike a similar cord when they argue that 'thinking sociologically is a way of understanding the human world that also opens up the possibility about thinking about the same world in a different way.'

Sociology took shape in Europe during a time of momentous social and economical change. Political change had expression in the French Revolution and with it came far reaching consequences (Willis 1999, p. 3). The two scientific revolutions, the seventeenth century and the late eighteenth and early nineteenth century, the latter referred to by Holmes as the 'Age of Wonder', saw an expansion in the wonders and reach of scientific developments (Holmes 2009). Scientific discoveries produced inventions which were to drive the new industries and change domestic lives and consumption patterns. These events brought about a complex changed world; a 'modern world', where people's everyday lives reflected change in the previous social and economic order.

Giddens notes that life changed dramatically due to this shift away from traditional roles. It was '...born of the transformation which wrenched the industrialising social order of the West away from the forms of life characteristic of pre-existing societies' (Giddens 1989, p. 2). De-traditionalisation therefore is argued to open up new possibilities for identity: whereas roles were once prescribed, they are now argued to have been freed up (Giddens 1991). Willis writes of this period:

It was associated with the transition over a substantial period in social, economic and political arrangements, and in the way with the various groups in society related to each other. The revolution consisted of two aspects: technological and social. (Willis 1993, p. 3)

The changes brought about through industrialisation and the rise of technologies has both permeated and been reflected in popular culture and the arts. The works of classic writers is an example. Charles Dickens published his book *The Tale of Two Cities,* a story about people living in London and Paris at the time of the French and Industrial Revolutions in 1859, two years after the death of the early sociologist Auguste Comte. The opening stanza of this classic text invokes the kaleidoscopic nature and consequences of these social, economic and technological changes.

It was the best of times,
it was the worst of times,

it was the age of wisdom,
it was the age of foolishness,
it was the epoch of belief,
it was the epoch of incredulity,
it was the season of Light,
it was the season of Darkness,
it was the spring of hope,
it was the winter of despair (Dickens 1859)

The Industrial Revolution generated progress for good and generated change for ill. Wealth was accumulated, new divisions of labour and new forms of workplaces emerged, home life and social communities changed significantly, and people moved from agricultural land and lifestyles to urban cities and urban living. It was the worst of times with inequality, hardship and dispossession. As raw commodities and new markets were sought around the globe, colonisation and dispossession of people from their lands, the rupture of kin networks, and discounting of traditional ways took place. The scale of industrial change in the Industrial Revolution and contemporary change due to the digital technological revolution was dramatically depicted by director Danny Boyle in the Opening Ceremony of the London 2012 Olympics, with the visual effects of rising chimneys, smoke plumes and speed of technological advance irrevocably changing the landscape.

As Willis (1999) describes, in this time of change, sociologists such as Auguste Comte, Emile Durkheim, George Simmel, Ferdinand Tönnies, Karl Marx and Max Weber were likely thinking: what had changed and what were the mechanisms of change? What were the underlying processes that constituted and maintained social institutions and social relations in the emerging worlds? How had these altered previous patterns of social life, of the attainment of wellbeing and lives of oppression? What could be a new world? How does one engage in social science investigations? Their theoretical and empirical work focused on different puzzles. Nisbet groups their preoccupations as concerns with '...community, authority, status, the scared and alienation' (Nisbet 1966, p. 6). Willis writes:

> Each in their own way attempted to make sense of the changes that were occurring around them. These changes were not only economic but also profoundly political and moral in character. The meaning and implications of these changes for how societies functioned was the subject of detailed analyses by these writers and thinkers. (1999, p. 3–4)

The lexicon associated with the writings of these sociological scholars demonstrates their intellectual differences and conceptual inventions. For example, Durkheim contributed insights on religious practices (Durkheim 1976 [1912]), social cohesion (Durkheim 1984 [1893]), solidarity and alienation, or what he named anomie (Durkheim 1952 [1897]), and social facts (Durkheim 1982 [1895]). Marx left an intellectual legacy on the relations of the productive economic base of a society to the superstructures of societal institutions and social relations; he theorised about alienation of people from nature and 'themselves' in their commodification in capitalism and dynamics of social change and revolution (McLellan 1971).

Weber left insights on work ethic and religion, industrialisation and rationality (Weber 1976 [1905]) with acute resonance to these current times (Lemert 2007). Tönnies formulated concepts that distinguish between types of social relations as '*gemeinschaft*' (community) and '*gesellschaft*' (society) and which are much cited in community sociology and community development.

Subsequent sociological thinkers have built upon the work of the 'classical sociologists'. They have extended analyses, for instance about solidarity and alienation; refuted claims and conceptual insights, illuminated omissions of race and gender, theorised on gender relations, race, emotions and intimacy, cultural and identity; and introduced new insights about the worlds they are thinking about. Sociology continues to evolve and is a rigorous and critical tradition in which new theorising and empirical work emerges.

Social Work Emerges

Into the nineteenth century world of industrial and social change and classical sociological inquiry, social work was emerging as a distinct and named undertaking. Social work was forged in the activities of both various charitable organisations, churches, philanthropic groups and fraternal societies and social reform movements like the Settlement Movement; the latter motivated by a value commitment to social justice. The charitable organisations gave practical assistance to meet needs and did so from a base in religious and moral conviction; that is, they provided shelter, food, safety and work to those who were homeless, cold, hungry and poor, and the victims of exploitation and injustice. They further had an education and remedial focus as their moral dispositions called them to skill up and 'reform the poor' and in cases help was proffered only to those deemed worthy of assistance (that is, the 'deserving poor'). As Lee says, it was 'Widows and children, the disabled, and the elderly [who] were gradually considered deserving' (Lee 1994, p. 41).

An example is the New York Children's Aid Society, who in their First Circular in 1853 outline their intention to form a society for 'destitute children', to '... give these work, and to bring them under religious influence...where they can learn an honest trade' (Pumphrey and Pumphrey 1961, p. 117). An explicit agenda was to prevent these children from future lives of crime and a reading of their circulars shows the lengths to which they engaged in activities to do this.

Social work was also concerned with social analysis and enduring social change as well as helping in the 'here and now'. For example, Jane Addams, a progressive social worker, co-founded Hull House, an early settlement house in the USA. She had drawn her inspiration from a wider settlement movement stirred by active organisations like Toynbee Hall in London founded in the late nineteenth century in Tower Hamlets and still active today as a community organisation. The principle of the settlement movement was that the social reformers resided amongst the people they were seeking to assist. Together they addressed issues and considered what needed to be done. In a way they were what we would now consider to be 'think tanks' or the incubators that were referred to earlier.

The actions of these social reformers, for example women like Jane Addams and her colleagues, reflect a perspective on social work. This is to engage directly and in relationship with the poor, with an embedded conviction that change could be brought about through support to people, to assist themselves but that it also needed change in the wider social order. In her writings and practice there is a clear view of the 'social' and the mechanisms of social change. Jane Addams was an articulate activist and with other social workers in 1915 participated in a mass action against the First World War, travelling to the Hague. She and other social workers and feminists formed the Women's International League for Peace and Freedom (WILPF), an organisation that still exists to this day (WILPF 1985).

It is important to note that Addams was a collectivist: her work is characterised by the understanding that to achieve change one must work with others towards a common social purpose. There was also a dialectical influence between sociologists and social workers at this time with key sociological figures such as Mead, Dewey and Cooley being connected to Addams' work (Forte 2004, p. 393). '[I]mportant social workers and symbolic interactionists encouraged each other, in the early part of the century, to promote social activism and democratization.' In 1917, for example, Mead, Dewey, and Addams marched down Chicago's Michigan Avenue in unified support of women's suffrage (Deegan and Burger 1978; Forte 2004, p. 393).

Given the varied work of charitable organisations and social reform movements, it is not surprising that in practice social work has always been rather difficult to narrow down, since it covers a wide range of activities (Payne 2005, p. 11) and has come from quite different antecedents. Depending on the ideological orientation of the social work writer, this purpose for social work has been described differently, for example, as a 'helping profession', 'mediating between the person and their environment', 'working to reform the behaviour of the person', 'supporting people adapt to their environment', 'working towards social justice', and 'advocating a new social order'.

Against this backdrop of ideological difference in the purpose of social work, social work is a practice endeavour, and the noun 'work' is salient. Social workers will be active with people and groups at times when their personal helping resources, or resources available in their support system (whether kinship, family or friends) are depleted; whether through sickness, or caring responsibilities, being out of paid work, or in low paid work and having the stress of not having adequate income to cover the costs of living, relationship or life challenges that come about as people move from one life stage or transition to another, or because they suffer discrimination and oppressive relations. Social workers assist people to access supports available through the state welfare systems or other sources of assistance, which are becoming more conditional and complex, as well as to assist in strengthening their own capabilities or resources. The nature of the work will be different in various settings, for example what the social worker does will be different in a hospital compared to when working with young people in a community setting.

This is, however, only one part of the picture, but this can be lost in the ways in which social work roles are delineated within agencies, and in social work education (Ife 1997, p. 196). Social work is about support for the development of a socially just society where people can realise social rights in the attainment of material and social wellbeing, health, social connectivity and participation. This view of social work is based on a moral and 'philosophical' grounding (Reamer 1993). Social work here has a focus on 'upstream work', in other words change in the situations that stop these rights from being people's direct experiences, and the social worker will use all sorts of strategies in this work.

There is a constant tension here between social work as an agent of the state, reinforcing social control objectives and dominant norms and values that maintain the status quo, and social work enacted in ways that contribute to a social change project. There is a range of views as to the order of societal change needed, as we will cover in this book. The ethical and moral responsibilities of the work are immense, and this speaks to our responsibility in being thinking social workers, for how otherwise can we claim to be contributing to empowerment and justice. Moreover it is incumbent on social workers to not inadvertently contribute to oppression and inequitable power relations, thinking all the while that we are working for social justice.

Ways of Seeing: Sociological Social Work

The use of sociology in social work is not a new phenomenon, as we explore throughout this book. There are books in social work which explore sociology *for* social work (Dominelli 1997; Cunningham and Cunningham 2008). Such texts highlight the importance of understanding the world through sociological theories. Dominelli argues (1997) that this knowledge – the understanding of sociological theories – can act as an inoculation against social workers becoming unthinking agents of the state. She names an approach called sociological social work. She writes:

> Sociological social work is what I call that form of social work practice which addresses directly the "politics of practice". It is founded on sociological understanding about the nature of society, human relationships, and social interactions, social institutions and power relationship, and the distribution of resources and opportunities. (Domenilli 1997, p.59)

There are other approaches which take a particular sociological approach and fuse it with social work practice, like structural social work (Mullaly 1997) and Ife's *Critical Practice* (1997). Ife (1997, p. 196) for example is clear that 'at the heart of social work' is a seamless link between the micro and the macro. Other writers like Schwartz have taken up C. Wright Mills' idea of a sociological imagination, and the need to consider the link between 'private pain and public trouble' (Schwartz 1974).

However, there has been difficulty in locating and articulating what social work informed by sociology might involve, let alone how we might find the words to articulate this kind of practice. Some of the difficulty in pinning down what might be sociological in relation to social work seems to stem from the shifting terrain in which we practice. The organisational and geographical contexts change – so too does our social world – and given the dynamic, spontaneous and experiential work we undertake in social work, it can be difficult to retain one particular lens.

There is a rich history of scholarship in which 'ways of seeing' (Berger 1977) are utilised as metaphors for learning and seeing the world in new ways. The connection between our visually experienced world and the words we use to describe it rely upon interpretation (Monaco 1981) which involves the application of theory and knowledge alongside experience and knowledge of society. This translates into social work. Judith Lee's 'fifocal vision', for example, involves the metaphor of a multifaceted lens with which social workers are urged to view the world around them and the work they undertake in practice (Lee 1994). The five lenses that Lee combines looks for the history of oppression, an ecological perspective, ethclass, feminist lens, and a critical perspective on power (Lee 2004).

The use of optical metaphors is common in social work and we draw on this, but use instead the optical image of the kaleidoscope, to symbolise what we call sociological social work and bring our approach to life. Kaleidoscopes are defined as follows:

Kaleidoscope: An optical instrument, consisting of from two to four reflecting surfaces placed in a tube, at one end of which is a small compartment containing pieces of coloured glass; on looking through the tube, numerous reflections of these are seen, producing brightly coloured symmetrical figures, which may be constantly altered by rotation of the instrument. (Oxford Dictionary 1973, p. 1146)

Each time the instrument is turned another composite view of coloured glass pieces appears. The possibilities to view are endless, yet there is a certainty in the form of the tube and the turning mechanism. This solid form symbolises the certainty of social work itself: social work values and its commitment to social justice and challenging oppression. For social workers there is certainty in the values, ethics and purpose that define social work. There is, however, a multiplicity of possibilities in how social work values and purpose will be exercised in practice and these will change with contexts, time/space and with the times. The kaleidoscope metaphor helps connect the world of experience with the concepts and words we use to describe our practice: in this way the kaleidoscope provides an addition to words and practice, something which is vital given our immersion in the social world around us.

Just as our contexts of practice change, so too can the kaleidoscope shift and alter and provide a new sociological theoretical lens through which we can view our work. Reconciling what we see with what we know can be challenging:

It is in seeing which establishes our place in the surrounding world; we explain that world with words, but words can never undo the fact that we are surrounded by it. The relation between what we see and what we know is never settled. (Berger 1977, p. 7)

We argue that sociological social work involves the deliberate utilisation of a sociological view of the world in which the individual is understood only in relation to their social contexts. There are a number of sociological theories which tackle the challenges put forward in contemporary life and we argue that social work misses an opportunity when it fails to view practice through the kaleidoscope. The image of a kaleidoscope is a useful metaphor to which the social worker can return. Just as the turning container or tube holds within the possibilities of different coloured glass patterns, there are a myriad of interests, interpretations and challenges in social work. Yet a constant, rather like the tube itself, is the relational nature of life: power relations and human inter-subjective relations. Both create patterns of ongoing oppressive elements and both are possible spaces for new developments to further a peaceful and socially just world.

Summary

In summary, the very nature of social work's mission requires attention to the social context in which people live and changing contexts raise many issues for social work. If practitioners are to be mindful of context and use this thinking to inform practice, then how is the current transforming context to be read and made sense of? What explanations about social relations and social change, and what explanations about the implications of change, both for now and for the future, are to be drawn upon? How can social workers work for social justice, beyond a practice where they are blinded to the complexities of the world in which they seek to change, and indeed claim to understand?

We suggest that sociological social work is a tool to aid this enterprise and that it can animate the central purpose of social work in ways relevant to the times and the forces and contexts that shape the times. Our approach builds on the existing work in establishing the currency of sociology to social work. We argue that sociological social work provides a legitimate name and perspective for a type of practice. Sociological social work is both a sensibility which requires imagination and knowledge, and it is a practice approach: these require literacy in sociology and social work. Sociological social work requires knowledge about sociological and social work theory and this book contains some of the key sociological and social work theories which help navigate our contemporary setting.

The Outline of Sociological Social Work

The book commences by examining the existing scholarship which is relevant to sociological social work. In understanding the historical conditions which give rise to our work, we argue that there is a unique opportunity for social work to engage in the social world with a renewed vigour.

In Chapter 2 we argue for the inclusion of a sociological kaleidoscope as a legitimate form of practice. The influence of sociology on the ways in which social work is practiced is argued to provide practitioners, scholars and educators in social work with a new way of working. Sociological social work involves two conditions: a sociological sensibility and a critical understanding of the world using sociological literacy in theory.

Chapter 3 examines the social work self. In understanding identity we need to engage in both the ways in which social work is understood by others as well as the ways in which social workers understand their own professional selves. In this chapter we explore performative theory of identity and apply the interactionist theory of self developed by George Herbert Mead to social work. Thus we make the case that sociological social work ought to both understand itself as well as the theories which are used to understand selfhood.

The interactionist tradition is argued to provide a theoretical foundation upon which the profession may construct further scholarship about selfhood (Dunk-West 2013). Rather than the self being a notion which emerges from the increasing individualisation which is argued to characterise late modern life (Giddens 1991), Mead's self is reliant upon sociality for its genesis (1913 [2011]; Mead 1925 [2011]; 1934). This belief that humans require social interaction is something which resonates in social work.

In Chapter 4 we examine the context in which social work takes place: namely, within the organisation. The organisational context to social work is central to the ways in which we think about the social work identity. In this chapter we use Weber's concept of the iron cage to make sense of neo-liberal ideals and the ways in which they thwart social work values and purpose. The management of risk is identified as one of the major drivers of service provision in that risk negatively influences both services provided as well as the ways in which social work is practiced. We argue that the application of Bourdieu's habitus and field, Weber's iron cage and contemporary theories of risk can help to draw out a sociological social work. This means retaining a broader perspective which understands risk as an historical condition rather than as something which limits agency, practice and services provided to others. A strong social work identity is crucial to this project which challenges the notion that welfare is under a neo-liberal project of individualisation. It is only through the maintenance of the historical and sociological understanding of this historical period that social workers can retain their core values and fight for the pursuit of social justice within the organisational context.

Chapter 5 explores social work values and ethics. We argue that the everyday level of analysis is important to understanding the ways in which the professional self is drawn from the identity lived in day-to-day life. It is the task of the social work student or practitioner to understand the connections or disconnections between their values. Values and ethical positions are developed through people's social situations, contexts and biographies and the social worker must connect their everyday ethics along with the ethical perspectives and values which drive the profession of social work. Social justice is identified as a central value in social work which can be used to underpin the work that we engage in. Understanding the global nature of contemporary life and the inequalities in relation to nation and aspects of difference such as gender, sexual identity, race, culture, age, (dis)ability and educational status helps to remain grounded in our changing world. We argue that a sociological social work in relation to ethics is one which employs theories that help us understand our social world and the historical and social forces which have a bearing on such a world.

In Chapter 6 we consider the role of communities and social relationships in social work. We argue that the meaning of community, though changing in a changing world, still retains importance in social work. Climate change and social solidarity is argued to be important concepts in contemporary social work practice in Chapter 7. We discuss some of the key issues in relation to our geographical contexts and use

In Chapters 8 and 9, we explore some of the key issues related to time and social work. In Chapter 8 we take up a focus on time and social work in a world where changes in technology are impacting experiences of time (Castells 1996; Melucci 1998). We write about time because it is, we suggest, a way into thinking sociologically, and especially to think about what we may not think about or take for granted in a changing social world. Opening a window in time is to open a window on the contours of social lives, the diversity of social experiences across life courses, and concurrent social worlds. In Chapter 9 we consider the ways in which changes in time and space affect social work. These chapters highlight the new ways in which we are relating to one another in an era where technologies are changing our communication methods and practices. We argue that greater theorising about time is crucial to social work scholarship. Without a critical engagement with new forms of relating, we are in danger of falling behind in innovative responses to the changing ways in which we relate to one another. Since relating to one another is a core skill to social work practice, time and space in late modernity ought to have a broader focus in our work.

In Chapter 10, social work and capitalism is examined. We demonstrate the disjunct between market models and social work ideals. The insurance industry is cited as an example of a profession which has become important to social work provision and is a reminder of the ways in which neo-liberal values pervade our work. Some of the key sociological theories relating to the critique of economic systems such as capitalism are discussed in this chapter.

Chapter 11 concludes *Sociological Social Work*. We note the themes of the changing world, new forms of relating and interacting and the importance of the ongoing commitment to social work values such as social justice. Sociological social work is summarised as being a valid and crucial theoretical foundation for practice; an essential sensibility for social workers and the way to highlight the 'social' in 'social work'.

Part 1
Subjective Identity, Self and Agency

Chapter 2
Building on Past Foundations

Two things fill my mind with ever new and increasing wonder and awe, the more often and persistently I reflect upon them; the starry heaven above me and the moral law within me...I see in front of me and unite them immediately with the consciousness of my own existence. (Immanuel Kant)

Introduction

This chapter is a brief historical sketching of traditions where a case has been made for sociological ideas to inform social work. A broad sweep of ideas and sociological reference points within social work will be covered. This includes the work of writers such as Harriet Bartlett (*The Common Base of Social Work Practice* 1970), William Schwartz (*One Social Work Job or Two* 1969), Jim Ife (*Critical Social Work* 1997) and Lena Dominelli (*Sociology for Social Work* 1997). The threads that connect their ideas, as well as their unique, distinctive contributions, will be drawn together. We also touch on those writers who have identified a particular set of ideas and used them as the foundational knowledge for a social work model of practice. As we outlined in Chapter 1, the main aim of this book is to provide students and practitioners with a way to think sociologically as a reference for informing and making sense of the world we practice in, the encounters they have with 'clients', groups and 'communities', and how they see and understand the signs of something new. It is this sensibility we suggest is needed to inform how social workers think, how they view the contexts in which they practice, make sense of the situations which mean that people need social work assistance, the intentions and strategies of their practice and themselves as practitioners.

Shifting Constellations

If you look upwards on a clear, light-free night, in wintertime in the northern hemisphere, and the summer evening sky in the south, you can make out the star constellation Orion, the hunter. Close by are his companion dogs, Canis Minor and Canis Major. To help you locate Orion you might look for the bright star Betelgeuse that marks out a shoulder, or perhaps you can recognise the star Rigel pinpointing Orion's leg, or the stars that make up Orion's belt, colloquially referred to as the saucepan. That this collection of stars forms the shape of a hunter, so named by the ancient Greeks, is one way to draw this star pattern.

There are other ways. The same group of stars were known by the Australian Indigenous Boorong people as '*Kulkunbulla* – the two young dancing men' (http://museumvictoria.com.au/Education/); ancient Syrian culture saw this star group to be a giant, and in ancient Mongolian culture the stars that we call Orion the hunter were animals (Heckert 2007). A hunter, a giant, dancing men and animals; across time, space and cultures different constellations have been made from the same points of light in the night sky.

In 1930 the International Astronomical Union (IAU), using the work of the astronomer Delporte, made official 88 heavenly constellations that were a selection amongst many options, giving preference to European traditions (IAU, http://www.iau.org/public/constellations/). Of course, this official star constellation status is a construct; it does not diminish that they are what humans interpreted to be the constellations of the night sky. Humans, as the star gazers, have been pattern makers and assigned visible stars to constellations and used culture and myths to create lively and engaging tales that enlighten of human and social experiences: stories of revenge, suffering, longing and redemption. In some ancient cultures the constellations played a role in earthly rituals, with symbolic significance. The depiction of the 'heavens' is an exercise in collective imagination, and it is reinforced through the wisdom of official astronomy experts, the star books we read and cultural myths. Michael Leunig, an Australian cartoonist, has designed a portrait of the night sky using contemporary daily experiences. His constellations are named 'condom in the carpark', 'upturned shopping trolley', 'small croissant', 'disillusioned feminist' and although a humorous illustration, his work highlights the ways in which we code the world around us using symbols and imagery from our cultural practices and beliefs. A more contemporary night sky for amateur astronomers to observe.

What has this to do with social work? The idea of a constellation as a metaphor for social work was directly employed in the 1950s by social workers in North America as an organising framework to unite the components of social work:

> Social work practice, like the practice of all professions, is recognized by a constellation of value, purpose, sanction, knowledge, and method. No part alone is characteristic of social work practice nor is any part described here unique to social work. It is the particular content and configuration of this constellation which makes it social work practice and distinguishes it from the practice of other professions...This implies that some social work practice will show a more extensive use of one or the other of the components but it is social work practice only when they are all present to some degree. (*Working Definition of Social Work Practice* 1958, in Bartlett 1970, p. 221)

Social work is comprised of a panorama of social work constellations each a unity of '...value, purpose, sanction, knowledge, and method'; as discussed in Chapter 1 this is not surprising given social work's mixed antecedents (Bartlett 1970; Dominelli 1997; Payne 2005; Healy 2005). There are constellations where, with greater brightness shine the theories and social work practices which fix the change project with individuals, and the knowledge roots are deep in psychological and psycho-analytic discourses (Bartlett, 1970; Healy, 2005, p. 49). Social work in this approach will use an interpretative lens that analyses the individual's situation, their capabilities and support systems, and perhaps how to address matters like how individuals can further their problem-solving capabilities, heighten psychological insights, resourcefulness and active agency.

In other social work constellations the change project is in reference to transforming social structures and social relations; this is founded in an imagination of new social relations and new social structures and radical change to the existing social order. This change project is in a realm beyond the actions or inactions of individuals, although individuals making change may well be part of the path to radical structural change. The social work analysis in such constellations is about how oppressive social relations and social structures impact the lives of people, communities and social systems, and what can be imagined and enacted so that things are differently structured to meet human needs and enable social wellbeing (Mullaly 1997; Ife 1997). Other constellations will view the order of change from a social reformist perspective and this is where social change is to 'temper and reform' the effects of capitalism and unjust social systems.

The gamut of social work constellations is because there are variations in social work ideologies and values, sanction, knowledge and method. Payne illustrates this in his grouping of social work theories into three larger clusters of ideas: reflexive-therapeutic views, socialist-collectivist views and individualist-reformist views (2005, pp. 8–9). Within varied fields of practice certain knowledge paradigms will take precedence over others; for example in health settings a medical model is dominant and this foregrounds and privileges medicalised causal explanations and solutions. In child welfare practice, attachment theories based in the work of John Bowlby and Mary Ainsworth have a firm hold and these are based in psychoanalytical theories about parent/child relations. The social work advocated by Mullaly is a political project to 'restructure society along socialist lines' (1997, p. 163) and practice attention is to see the link of the personal to the political, work for empowerment and consciousness raising and a broader project of collective action. In outlining his theoretical approach he draws upon Marxist, Feminist and neo-Marxist thinkers in critiquing capitalist social systems and he argues that '...structural social workers seek to change the social system and not the individuals who receive, through no fault of their own, the results of defective social arrangements' (1997, p. 133).

In the course of history social work constellations are made and remade, reflecting the drifts in knowledge debates and knowledge production, and the connections between social work and dominant societal responses to social and political conditions. For instance, changes in the institutional mandate for social work will change as governments change and certain practices will be retrenched and others elevated in their importance. In other words what social workers are required to do by the government services and non-government bodies that employ them will change with public policy settlements. This has been profoundly significant in the dominance of neo-liberal-inspired governments in OECD countries and the redefinition of the social work role. Related is the fact that social workers occupy posts that cross a huge span of areas and there is considerable diversity in the subjective experiences, biographies, needs and interests of the people with whom we work.

As we outlined in Chapter 1, the main aim of this book is to provide students and practitioners with a way to think sociologically as an anchor and reference for interpretation, analysis, deliberation and action in accordance with values based social work practice. It is this sensibility that we suggest is needed to equip social workers with the conceptual tools, literacy and discernment to make sense of the complex and dynamic circumstances which bring people into contact with social work and to support empowering change. We argue sociological social work to be a powerful support to what is an incredibly challenging mandate and to deepen reflexive insights. A sociological sensibility is a way to integrate, as an on-going process, conceptual and action domains; to have a social analysis congruent with social work values and purpose, and clear conceptual maps to shore up the social worker in the work they do.

The social work constellations that we focus on in this chapter are ones where arguments have been made for sociological ideas to inform social work. These arguments emerge from varied standpoints and have different routes. There is a tradition spelling out sociological knowledge for social work; knowledge about social theories of power, social relations, institutions, community and family, gender and race. Indeed all social work students will likely study some sociology in their degrees. There are other approaches which present sociological knowledge relevant to a setting or functional area, for example the sociology of food and nutrition (Germov and Williams 1999) and health and medical sociology (Cheek et al. 1996). Yet other approaches integrate sociological ideas into the approach to social work: William Schwartz (1969), Jim Ife (1997) and Lena Dominelli (1997) are authors in this tradition. The threads that connect their ideas, as well as their unique distinctive contributions, will be drawn in this chapter and how this book builds on these existing foundations.

Looking to the Past – the Case for Sociological Social Work

One of the ongoing deliberations amongst social workers and academics has been about the core of social work knowledge for practice. In 1921, Porter Lee from the New York School of Social Work raised the following question at a Social Work Conference: 'How can you describe a social worker so that he (sic) can be distinguished from someone else? What does a social worker know?' (cited in Pumphrey and Pumphrey 1961, p. 311). Not only is there debate about the 'knowledge base' of social work, there are also competing views on the focus and form of social work methods and intervention (Healy 2005), or the ideological form of the constellation.

There are a number of foundational social work texts that give grounding in the richness of sociological thinking and introduce sociology theory and themes. Anne Llewellyn, Lorraine Agu and David Mercer in their book *Sociology for Social Workers* (2008) provide this broad sociological overview to support the social worker in their thinking and practice. They write:

> It is important that social workers understand the social conditions and processes within which they operate and sociology offers theories to understand these processes and the nature of the social world in which they inhabit. (2008, p. 2)

Llewellyn et al. cover material such as sociological concepts of power, globalisation, key sociological theories expounded by the classical and more contemporary sociologists (structural theories, conflict theories, social action theories, feminist and anti-racist theories) and follow this overview with in-depth consideration of sociological ideas in the areas of social class and poverty, gender, race and sexuality, ethnicity, family and change, health and life-course periods.

There are other writers whose works have been significant in the social work tract, in that they have propounded the case to integrate knowledge, and this to support the social worker gain greater competence in addressing issues for the individual with a mindset about the context of the environment. In practice this also means attention to change in the environment, defined as a broad social, political and economic context. The work of Harriet M. Bartlett, author of a classic book called the *Common Base of Social Work Practice,* which was first published in 1970, is an example.

Bartlett explores the fundamental distinctiveness of social work, a subject that was the focus of debate and thinking through the North American National Association of Social Workers (NASW) that took place through the late 1950s and the 1960s. She traces these and sets out a way to describe an integrative social work practice, or as Bartlett writes, the book '...is not a description of practice or an analysis of practice but rather a consideration of social workers' *ways of thinking* about their practice' (1970, p. 10). This includes taking on theoretical ways of thinking and relating this to social work concepts. Bartlett reflects on her observation that social workers have a reticence to engage in theory and a lack of certainty about social work knowledge, a theme noted in more recent works (Mullaly 1997; Domenilli 1997). She argues, and considers the need for it to be readdressed, that social work practice experience and knowledge, or 'practice wisdom', rarely contributes to theory development. As she writes:

> Social workers have perhaps not given enough thought to the point that theoretical knowledge may actually be the most useful kind to possess in a rapidly changing society. (1970, p. 109)

The backdrop for Bartlett and her colleagues was a motivation to be part of the changes needed to respond to the social issues of the times, that is, 'civil rights, the urban crisis, poverty' (1970, p.13), as well as to the direct needs of the people with whom social workers were engaged. Bartlett articulates the conundrum that social workers will be constrained in fulsome enactment of a macro social work role if they do not have a means to think comprehensively about social worlds, and to think about social work as a profession. In Bartlett's own words:

> After half a century of exploring various forms of service, social workers are now able for the first time to perceive clearly the wide scope of their potential service. After prolonged concentration on work with individuals and small groups, the profession has been roughly jolted by the sudden recognition of urgent social problems, and the emergence of proliferating health and social welfare programs. In exploring anew their contribution to poverty, delinquency, urban development, and similar social problems, social workers can no longer work within the confines of their own agencies and at their own pace, but must be ready to work through new channels...Innovation is in the air and flexibility is a pre-requisite. (1970, p.15)

The NASW *Working Definition of Social Work* spelt out what distinguishes social work from other 'helping professions'. This is grounded in a value base from which social work purpose, knowledge and method spring. In other words the social work constellation is held together by values. The NASW expounds these values to be that the 'individual is the primary concern of this society', interdependence, social responsibility, the fulfilment of human needs and potential, the uniqueness of each person, active democratic participation and the role of society in enabling the realisation of human potential. In this social work constellation '...person and situation, people and the environment, are encompassed in a single concept, which requires they be constantly viewed together' (Bartlett 1970, p. 116).

One of the central thrusts of Bartlett's book is that social work is better served with an integrative knowledge base, a holistic approach where the whole transforms the component parts; rather than a knowledge base that consists of selective borrowing from a range of other fields, whether this is from psychological/psychoanalytical traditions or the social sciences. Throughout her book is an emphasis on building and consolidating this foundational base and moving beyond 'borrowing' from other fields. This knowledge base as Bartlett argues, needs to include knowledge of social functioning and social interactions or exchange and the impacts of the social environment on people's lives: 'It was the failure to bring the ideas of people and environment together and hold them there that produced such a long lag in social work thinking' (Bartlett 1970, p. 102).

Bartlett's points about the usefulness of theory, together with integrative practices, have direct relevance to the approach to sociological social work we outline in this book. The terms 'integration', 'integrative processes', 'integrative practices' and 'integrative thinking' are again popular, as seen in a number of diverse fields; psychotherapy, psychology, science, interdisciplinary education, health, economics, organisational theory and management, business, social policy and social planning. They tend to be referring to practices where the intention is to draw together ways to think about complex issues, for instance how to think about change in times that are uncertain and in a flux. Integrative approaches imply a level of critical analysis, dialogue and relational engagement and generative processes, out of which something new or transformational can emerge; the thesis being that 'the whole is greater than the sum of its parts', whether this be ideas and knowledge, resources, capabilities, imaginations and fears or functional areas (i.e. education and health). Green and McDermott (2010) take up the theme of social work's need to embrace complexity theory and to work in integrative ways in order to better respond to the 'evolving complexity' that marks our times.

The language of integration permeates all major government functional areas (e.g. health, housing, education, community welfare, water policy, environment etc.) in many countries, Australia and the United Kingdom included. There are integrated models for service delivery, social and land use planning, expectations for integration in welfare, education, health care provision, between levels of hospital and community care, as a tool for preventative health and so on. Such efforts for integration are a rejoinder to the policy and public management trends of the last 30 years, which have both paradoxically cemented public policy silos and fragmented delivery systems. This situation, in turn, some would argue, has made addressing complex social issues that much harder. It has impeded a capacity to think and respond holistically, to innovate whilst holding complexity in mind and to utilise, effectively, public and community resources. Perhaps more fundamentally, cemented silos negate the social whole and what is experienced holistically in families, communities and in individual lives and collective efforts to attain educational outcomes, health and wellbeing.

Yet, as history has repeatedly shown, discourses of such broad uptake can be no more than rhetoric producing superficial outcomes. Payne (2001) canvasses some of the barriers to integrative processes: political turf wars, rigid adherence to theoretical ideas and knowledge paradigms, privileging of certain ideas, organisational practices that keep silos in their place, group think, and lack of time to think in other ways. He balances the ledger with practical techniques for the facilitation of integrative processes: 'dialectical or devil's advocate approaches for planning' to reveal and challenge what may be deeply-held values, views and beliefs and various modes of 'thinking together approaches' (2001, p. 156). A further characteristic of this approach is the commitment to draw together different disciplinary approaches in recognition that silo ideas and practices will not suffice to address the challenges of complex social change and social problems that are inherently multi-dimensional.

It is the challenges wrought in current social change that set the context for Lena Dominelli's book *Sociology for Social Workers* (1997). She prefaces her argument with an appeal for '...a calm analysis that enables us to evaluate what is happening in social work practice and make decisions about its future direction' (1997, p. 1). This call is set against what she contends is a crisis in social work, marked by a pull into social control work, and confusion about social work identity and social work direction. This necessitates 'the revalidation and reclaiming' of social justice values based social work. Her social work constellation draws together the intellectual ideas and a critical practice for anti-racist, feminist social work, wherein considerations of the workings of power, oppression, and structural inequalities are fundamental. As with Bartlett, her focus is on an integrated knowledge base and the insights sociological theories and thinking can offer to social work analyses of societal conditions and what is best to be done for the people for whom social workers work.

Domenilli too identifies that 'social workers appear to have a dread of abstract theory which seems tangential to practice' (1997, p. 51). She is directly concerned with articulating sociology for social work that can be integrated into practice and that social workers make this approach a 'routine part of their practice' (1997). A living grasp of sociological concepts like power, gender and race relations and the institutional forms in which they are maintained and through which oppression continues, is essential. Domenilli passionately invokes the need for sociological social work as a means through which social workers can be agents in the realisation of an alternative social vision (2007, p. 240), and moreover, that this social work approach requires a way to think about '...the interactions between people and nature and among people' (1997, p. 247).

It is usual in social work writings of the later part of the twentieth century to read some reference to the ideas of the American sociologist C. Wright Mills, who wrote a seminal work entitled the *Sociological Imagination* (Schwartz 1969; Mullaly 1997). As referred to earlier Mills developed a way to think sociologically and to do so by switching on an imagination as a habitual thinking mechanism. Imagination as a 'quality of mind' is a capacity to do mental gymnastics, or to move from one sphere of thought to another and to use the phrase by Kant 'unite them immediately with the consciousness of my own existence.' In Mills' schema this imagination is a conceptual ability to think about individuals or human biographies, and the societal, and their interactions, and to do this in history time. In a set of questions he provides the keys to activate and sustain this imagination. Mills (1979) argues that those who exercise a sociological imagination ask these sorts of questions:

- What is the structure of this sort of society as a whole? What are its essential components and how do they relate to each other?
- Where does this society stand in human history? What are the mechanisms by which it is changing? How does it differ from other periods?
- What varieties of men and women now prevail in this society and in this period?
- And what varieties are coming to prevail? (1979, p. 13)

To exercise this form of intellectual activity allows connections and patterns to be drawn and insights gained. It allows for issues that are 'private pains' to be placed as 'public troubles' rather than be situated as just the responsibilities or inadequacies of humans. It also means seeing the rich and diverse expressions of human life; women and men, people of all races and ages, abilities, sexual identity, geographic locations and economic class. Thinking in this way means that a social worker will see the presenting issues and intervention beyond just an individualised or psychological conceptualisation; they will make patterns, rather like generations have made maps of the celestial heavens.

Consider the following example. Increasingly there has been a concerted global and national effort to respond to statistics that show that people are increasing in weight (OECD 2012) and to the resultant health problems. The OECD report that '...in 19 of 34 OECD countries the majority of the population is now overweight or obese' (2012, p. 1). In some countries this is especially so for children and young people, as is the case in Australia. Opinions are divided about what causes obesity, although there is a convergence of views that the causes are incredibly complex, involving not just what humans do and do not do but the worlds they live in. International experts write in the Medical Journal the *Lancet*: 'The number of suggested interventions, plus the contested nature of potential solutions, can create a 'policy cacophony', which makes the task of obesity prevention hopelessly difficult' (Gortmaker et al. 2011, p. 839). Because of this complexity interventions need to be multifaceted.

Interventions are recognised as necessary across a wide range from individual behaviour changes to the social context of food provision. This includes the quality, availability and affordability of food. Ward et al. (2013), in a study about access and supply of healthy foods, report that people from low income areas confront a range of financial stressors, which make affording a healthy basket of food extremely difficult. This type of research evidence shows the significance of needing to have enough money to afford the costs of healthy food, and if we think more about this, and ask why is this so, further lines of inquiry open up about the pricing and supply of food, about the interests, operations and profit motivations of the food industry, marketing of fast food, the location of food outlets in localities and the adequacies of incomes and benefits given the costs of living. Such thinking shows a way to change.

Bauman and May (2001) write:

> The art of sociological thinking is to widen the scope and practical effectiveness of freedom. When more of it has been learnt, the individual may well become just a little less subject to manipulation and more resilient to oppression and control. They are also more likely to be more effective as social actors, for they can see the connections between their actions and social conditions, and how these things, which by their fixity, claim to be irresistible to change are open to transformation. (2001, p. 11)

There are common threads in the works mentioned throughout this chapter. First is the need for social workers to develop a theoretical literacy and use theoretical concepts in an integrative way in their practice. Secondly, that central in this thinking are the dynamic links and interactions between individuals and the social structures in which they live, including what happens because of these interactions. Thirdly, that this approach is vital in contemporary worlds that are complicated, moving along and changing quickly, and when for too many people, there are deep inequalities, injustices and hardship. Essentially this is a sociological project (Giddens 1989). But the social work constellation calls for this knowledge to be held together with the values, purpose and method of social work.

Further Reading

Bauman, Z. and May, T. (2001) *Thinking Sociologically.* Oxford: Blackwell Publishing.

Dominelli, L. (1997) *Sociology for Social Work.* Basingstoke: Palgrave Macmillan.

Mills, C.W. (1970) *The Sociological Imagination.* Harmondsworth: Penguin.

Chapter 3
The Social Work Self

Imagine a social worker in a social situation outside of work. This social worker works in the area of child protection. It has been a difficult day as they have been in court giving evidence in a high profile case. Let us say that in this scenario they are at a party, talking to new people. The topic of conversation turns towards work. The social worker's heart rate increases, as they take in the knowledge that someone is about to ask them what they do for a living. The social worker looks around to see if they can make a quick escape from the party. They find it difficult to focus on the people around them as their thoughts turn to consider whether to tell these new friends that they are a social worker. The social worker looks frantically around. Is there someone else with whom they might strike up a conversation? Will the host be offended at a premature departure? It is too hard to gauge whether disclosure of the profession will result in a snide comment, a judgemental look or verbal abuse or worse. It could go any way. The social worker makes their way to the door.

Our scenario is a fictional one but highlights some of the tensions associated with the identity of 'social worker'. The way in which individuals experience their professional identities is influenced by attitudes and beliefs held by those around them. Stigma associated with social work can depend on the national context and our example draws from a British context. Yet negative attitudes can affect the experience of the profession and, importantly, influence the perception of other allied professionals, employers and crucially, clients. This can be particularly the case for social workers who work in areas in which there is a great deal of public scrutiny such as in child protection. The ways in which social workers are depicted and 'read' by others depends upon many factors such as the specific area of work or specialism, the national context and the current public mood. It is fair to say, for example, that social workers have received negative press in the British media in recent years. Here is a small selection of headlines from the *Daily Mail* which feature social workers:

Social worker took the wrong child out of primary school for a supervised visit with another child's father. (*Daily Mail*, 11 February 2013)

Social workers took away our baby for nine months: With no evidence against them, couple were banned from looking after their son. (*Daily Mail*, 23 March 2012)

My adoptive dad abused me for years but social workers ignored my complaints because he's gay. (*Daily Mail*, 28 March 2013)

These headlines may, of course, highlight injustices, however, for the purpose of this chapter we are considering social work identity and the ways in which it is framed in popular media. In this way, these headlines can therefore help by serving as cultural signifiers of the ways in which social work is reported in popular print media. In as little as three headlines we can see an image of the social worker beginning to emerge. Social workers are depicted as making unnecessary mistakes, careless, interfering without just cause, allowing abuse to occur and being politically correct to the detriment of the truly vulnerable.

Following a tragic child death from abuse, the *Sun* newspaper in Britain painted a social worker as negligent, lazy, careless and 'to blame' for the child's death: claims which were later challenged through the courts. The following is taken from the *Guardian* which reported on the case which ultimately led to the *Sun* issuing an apology and paying compensation to the social worker in question:

Sylvia Henry, a social worker in the London borough of Haringey for 23 years, was accused in articles published in the *Sun* of being "grossly negligent" in her handling of Peter Connelly's case and that she was "thereby to blame for his appalling abuse and death", the high court heard.

Henry's solicitor, Daniel Taylor, told Mr Justice Eady the newspaper also said she had shown no remorse for these failings and was "shameless and had ducked responsibility for Peter's death".

In a series of articles published over four months from November 2008, the *Sun* also alleged that Henry was lazy and "had generally shown an uncaring disregard for the safety of children, even in cases where they obviously required urgent protection".

The false allegations are understood to have been published in about 80 articles and Henry was also named in the *Sun's* Justice for Baby P campaign, which called for Haringey social services staff it alleged were responsible for Connelly's death to be sacked and barred from any future work with children. The *Sun* gathered 1.6m signatures for its petition, which was delivered to Downing Street. Taylor said the newspaper "unreservedly accepts that there is no justification for any of the allegations". (Jason Deans, the *Guardian*, 'The *Sun* makes payout to social worker over Baby P stories', 9 June 2011)

A sustained stream of negative press stories points to social workers as needlessly removing children from their families, overly bureaucratic and ineffectual, and as failing at protecting the truly vulnerable. Although such media reportage rarely tells the 'whole' story, it can help to better understand the social context in which they proliferate. Social workers often work with people experiencing disadvantage, marginalisation and oppression. The work takes place between individuals, groups and communities and often the nature of the work means that there is a lack of public knowledge about what social workers do unless people encounter social work in their day-to-day lives or media.

Social workers, particularly in child protection for example, are often unable to publicise their triumphs. Children who have been taken into care and removed from abusive families ought to have their privacy upheld and respected by those who work with them, which prevents their story becoming a very public news item. People who have come into contact with social workers, for example, to work to resolve homelessness, may be understandably reluctant to talk to others about their experience. Individual interactions between a social worker and their client may be discussed by the client in individualised ways. For example, a client may say 'Jane really helped me when I needed it', which is vastly different to media portrayal of the profession.

Recently formed, The College of Social Work aims to address the overly negative press that social work and social workers receive in England. They aim to do this through promoting social workers and their clients telling positive stories about the work that they do (see www.tcsw.org.uk).

Importantly, it is crucial to note that in media reporting social workers are often depicted as being responsible for harming others. In such negative stories, the perpetrators of violence and abuse against children are often merely background to reportage in which social workers are portrayed as responsible for tragedies such as child deaths. This highlights one of the ways in which social workers are conveyed as having to 'take responsibility' for a child's death or harm, rather than the perpetrator themselves.

However, international variations exist in the ways in which 'social work' is created in national contexts. A social worker working as a mediator or family counsellor in Australia may have a completely different experience, as may a hospital social worker in the United States of America. The child protection worker will work predominantly with people who are poor and disadvantaged whereas a counsellor may work with people across a range of income levels. This may have something to do with the 'respectability' of the profession (G. Spolander pers comm) and the ways in which social work is 'coded' through labelling processes. Sociology can help with articulating an understanding of the broader story of social work – its discourse – in order to draw out the meaning behind unnecessarily negative stereotypes of social workers.

In this chapter we have looked at two examples, the first detailing a scenario where a social worker is, in a social situation, unsure of whether to tell new acquaintances about their profession, the other the role of the media in building up a negative image of social workers. Both of these are important when thinking about social work identity, not least because they tell us something about the ways in which social work is viewed by others. The external image or identity of social work impacts upon *social workers* themselves.

In the first scenario it was what was unsaid which caused consternation. In the case of some of the media in England, it is the case of what is said and how stories of abuse and neglect are framed. How do these play in to one's identity as a social worker? In this chapter we consider the meaning of the social work self from both the perspective of others as well as from the perspective of the social worker.

In understanding how the social work self is constituted, questions arise relating to the role of agency and reflexivity and the ways in which the professional self is connected with other selves social life. In this chapter we argue that social work is yet to develop a real engagement with theories of identity or selfhood (Dunk-West 2013). In contributing to this project, we explore two related ideas which resonate through sociology: the idea of selfhood as performative and the interactionist account of identity. We argue that the interactionist account of self, as offered by Mead, successfully accounts for the complexities inherent in the social work self. In particular, the application of Mead's interactionist self to social work (Dunk-West 2013) is advanced in this chapter. In adopting an interactionist framework to social work selfhood, we explore the synergy between the personal and the professional; the manifestation of identity in the social work task of assessment and reflexivity in relation to self-making. Given the prominence of the psychologically-defined notion of consciousness in popular and scientific cultural spheres (Furedi 2004), it is perhaps unsurprising that social work has failed to take up social models of selfhood in recent times. Yet Mead's interactionist theory of self highlights relationships and social relations, communication and socialisation which are all compatible with social workers' core business. Before examining Meadian selfhood in closer detail, let us now turn towards alternative theories of identity in which the role of society is central.

Performance and Performative Selves?

Goffman's self is one explained through his dramaturgical analysis. For Goffman, the self is externally projected and this activity is undertaken each moment and in every social situation. During social interaction, actors engage in 'impression management' in which their performance to their audience is geared towards creating a particular impression:

> When an individual appears before others, he knowingly and unwittingly projects a definition of the situation, of which a conception of himself is an important part. When an event occurs which is expressively incompatible with this fostered impression, significant consequences are simultaneously felt in three levels of social reality, each of which involves a different point of reference and a different order of fact. (Goffman 1959, p. 235)

Goffman argues that when one's performance is thwarted by an event resulting in 'performance disruptions'; the three areas which are affected are…personality, interaction and social structure (p. 236). In this way, the preservation of the performance helps all three of these levels interacting with one another.

One of the areas where the concept of performance, and in particular, performativity, is helpful is in understanding gender. Whereas one's sex is related to biological differences between males and females, gender points to the power of society to construct categories into which people are expected to fit. Here Goffman cites Simone de Beauvoir's analysis of the role of the social (and corporeal) in shaping identity:

> Even if each woman dresses in conformity with her status, a game is still being played: artifice, like art, belongs to the realm of the imaginary. It is not only that girdle, brassiere, hair-dye, make-up, disguise body and face; but that the least sophisticated of women, once she is "dressed", does not present herself to observation; she is, like the picture or the statue, or the actor on the stage, an agent through whom is suggested someone not there – that is, the character she represents, but is not. It is this identification with something unreal, fixed, perfect as the hero of a novel, as a portrait or a bust, that gratifies her; she strives to identify herself with this figure and thus to seem to herself to be stabilized, justified in her splendor. (de Beauvoir cited in Goffman 1959, p. 65)

Gender and performativity is developed in Judith Butler's work (Butler 1990). Whereas studies in subjectivity draw from a particular ontological understanding in which the notion of the pre-social mind is maintained, Butler's work around gender works to both unhinge and disrupt assumed categories and ontological assumptions (Nayak and Kehily 2006, p. 460). Nayak and Kehily explain how Butler does this:

> …Butler is driven by a radical impulse, not only to complicate and multiply identity formations by recognizing difference across time and space…but, above all, to subvert and implode the very basis of identity itself. This involves much

more than the deconstruction of gender into its socially constitutive parts as either masculine or feminine. It entails the stark recognition that the seemingly knowable sex categories of "male" and "female" are themselves fundamentally unstable discursive productions that in effect serve to make masculinity and femininity intelligible. (Nayak and Kehily 2006, p. 460)

Butler argues that instead of the focus being upon 'gender identity', in fact we ought to better understand that our everyday behaviours and interactions produce gender itself rather than the other way around (Butler 1990, p. 24). Nayak and Kehily found in their research that Butler's theory of gender can help to understand the ways in which individuals are able to subvert homophobia in the school setting (Nayak and Kehily 1996).

Theorists for whom identity is best understood through questioning the categories in which the term created is useful to social work practice, but important for social workers to understand. Such intellectual work helps to remind us that identity depends upon the ways in which we code activities and behaviours and that the ways in which we interact produce categories. Rather than accepting that a given label indicates a particular category, it is important to disrupt our assumptions and seek to better understand the role of the label itself and question its fixity. At the beginning of this chapter we began to examine some of the assumptions about social workers' identities which have been projected in media narratives. Whilst these are important to recognise – and most social workers would no doubt be aware of the view of their society about their work – it also raises the question of identity itself. Why is it important and how might we understand it in relation to social work? In this next section we move on to consider in some detail George Herbert Mead's theory of self. Mead's theory of self has been applied to social work and argued as relevant to understanding both ourselves as social workers as well as the people with whom we work (Dunk-West 2013).

George Herbert Mead's Self

George Herbert Mead's theory of self was noted in Chapter 1 of this book in relation to his work alongside Jane Addams in promoting social reform. Mead (1863–1931) was an American scholar based at the University of Chicago. His scholarship is associated with the symbolic interactionist tradition in sociology. Unlike other sociological approaches which highlight broader systems and social forces, symbolic interactionism is 'a theoretical approach in sociology developed by Mead, which places strong emphasis on the role of symbols and language as core elements of all human interaction' (Giddens 2005, p. 700). In this way, symbolic interactionism argues that we can learn about the world around us by studying interactions between individuals and groups. Everyday exchanges are the focus of some kinds of empirical work in this tradition, for example, the results of which are then related to broader knowledge and theories which relate to both the individual and the social world to which they belong (see, for example, Dunk-West 2012; 2011).

As we shall see, Mead highlights the centrality of social interaction to self-production. He argues that rather than the mind being associated with an internal quality, it cannot exist outside social interaction. Mead says that during childhood we learn about the 'rules' of social conduct. He argues that the self can only emerge through sociality (Mead 1913): this is an idea which has resonance for social work identity.

It is important to note the dialogical influence between Mead's early pragmatism and early social work figures (Maines 1997; Forte 2004, p. 393; Shaw 2011, p. 16) because it highlights the synergy between this kind of sociology and social work practice, theory and activism. Mead's emphasis on the social exchanges made in day-to-day life resonate through symbolic interactionism which sees these 'micro' exchanges as revealing key knowledge about our social world.

The location of the mind *outside* of the body highlights the centrality of what Mead calls social acts (Mead 1925) in everyday life. Thus, the alignment of psychological frameworks with notions of consciousness is to the detriment of the social. He argues that:

> The central nervous system has been unwittingly assimilated to the logical position of consciousness. It occupies only an important stage in the act, but we find ourselves locating the whole environment of the individual in its convolutions. (Mead 1925, p. 72)

The ways in which social workers view others *as well as themselves* ought to be given more prominence in social work literature. Somewhat uncritically, social work theory tends towards therapeutic-based notions of self which is often a result of pedagogical choices and curriculum design (Fook 1991). Generally, we believe that since the therapeutic notion of self dominates public life (Furedi 2004), social workers are more likely to replicate this preference in relation to the way that they conceptualise their professional selves.

Thinking about the subjective or individual self in social work is a useful starting point. For example, what frames of reference do social workers utilise in their everyday practices? How do social workers understand their own subjectivities? We agree that the interactionist tradition has been the victim of the social work profession's 'amnesia' (Forte 2004b, p. 521). Though strands of scholarship which draw together interactionism and social work continue to make their way into the literature, a clearer theoretical pathway must be borne out in the social work scholarly canon.

Let us return to what we have described as the 'subjective' social worker. We use the term subjective not to denote a psychoanalytically theorised identity, but to differentiate the individual social worker from their profession. Individual social workers, throughout their everyday social practices, view the world through the kaleidoscope of social work literature which encompasses practice knowledge, scholarship and research.

Yet the kaleidoscope is also infused with broader social meanings: the meanings derived from socialisation processes to engagement in contemporary social life and culture. Given, then, the diffusion of the ways in which individual life is made sense of using psychological ways of thinking about the self, is it any wonder that the kaleidoscope contains fragments of which the viewer is unaware? These fragments form through the immersion of the social worker in the society within which she or he is embedded.

In examining social work scholarship about reflexive learning, for example, this preference is revealed. We propose that Mead's interactionist self, constituted through social relationships, lessens the emphasis on reflexivity as the means through which professionals realise their social work selves. We now move on to consider reflexivity in more detail.

The Role of Reflexivity in Mead's Self and Social Work

Reflexivity is argued to be so prevalent in contemporary life that we are said to be constantly thinking about ourselves and how we might make ourselves 'better' (Giddens 1992, p. 30). This argument contends that there are various social forces which have come together which make for the 'extended reflexivity' (Adams 2003) that we see in day-to-day life. One example of the impacts new forms of reflexivity have had upon everyday interactions is the changing nature of our intimate or sexual relationships (Giddens 1992). Whereas once tradition tied people together in marriage, a new kind of reflexivity, in which we ask ourselves: 'am I happy in this relationship?', has brought about changes in the duration and nature of intimate partnerships (Giddens 1992).

Some social theorists interested in identity cite relationship breakdown as evidence of the deterioration of social life brought about by unstable modern conditions. For example, in modern social life actors are argued to have broken free from community and tradition, and are subsequently more interested in making individualised choices. This is argued to be to the detriment of intimate relationships because commitment no longer equates to lifelong partnerships. Bauman (2003, p. viii) asserts that broader social changes have encouraged this lack of commitment and dissatisfaction with intimacy. We are argued to be part of a new generation of actors for whom identity has become an 'ongoing project' (Giddens 1992, p. 30). Like Bauman, the link between late modern conditions and the nature of contemporary partnership patterns is assumed. Giddens theorises intimacy merely as part of a broader pattern in which individuals are increasingly faced with choices relating to identity production and continual, voluntary adjustment. Therefore, an individual's sexual self is not only part of their broader identity but is affected by the ubiquitous move towards increasing self-awareness. As Giddens (1992, p. 30) says, '[t]he question is one of sexual identity but not only this. The self today is for everyone a reflexive project – a more or less continuous interrogation of past, present and future.' We shall examine time in further detail in Chapters 9 and 10 of this book, however, it is important to note that periodisation scholars are interested in theorising identity through an analysis of this current epoch; named differently as 'late modernity' (Giddens 1992) or 'liquid modernity' (Bauman 2000) however they conflate everyday life with broader social shifts. The overemphasis on reflexivity within periodisation theories is not without contention because such analyses undervalue the importance of everyday social life. As Heaphy (2007, p. 4) notes:

> The reconstructivist theory of reflexive modernity proposed by Giddens and Beck, for example, has argued the emergence of new universalities and commonalities in global and individualized experience where there are no "others". This argument may be (relatively) convincing when it is focused on the abstract theoretical working out of the "reflexivity" of modernity, but it fails to be convincing when the theory is brought down to earth and compared to other arguments about how otherness and difference are centrally important – locally and on a global scale – to shaping personal and day-to-day experience, and to strategies of power.

Both Bauman (2003) and Giddens (1992) argue that the characteristics of the late modern world, such as globalisation, have enormous implications for the everyday interactions in people's social worlds. For Giddens however, the notion of reflexivity is not merely descriptive of the fact of being aware of oneself; rather, it extends beyond the individual. Broad economic and social changes are positioned as explaining the new 'transformatory' ways in which actors interrelate in their personal relationships during their day-to-day lives. Overemphasis on broader society to understand reflexivity does little to account for everyday social and cultural practices (Adams 2003). Indeed, the assumption that globalising forces have prompted increased reflexivity tends to split tradition and post-tradition (Alexander 1995). The problem with this dichotomy is the underlying assumption that tradition is relatively simplistic compared to the complex post-traditional life (Alexander 1995).

Why is Reflexivity Important to Social Work?

In social work, reflexivity has been highlighted as crucial to professional self-formation. Unlike in sociology, there is no recent orientation towards a critique of reflexivity. Rather, although there has been some theory building in relation to reflexivity and social work practice (Carey and Foster 2011; Fook 1999; Kessl 2009; Lam et al. 2007; Longhofer and Floersch 2012; Ferguson 2001; 2002; 2009; 2008), the role of reflexivity in social work education remains largely unchallenged. This is predominantly the case in relation to knowledge acquisition about the theory of practice.

The integration of theory into practice incorporates ideas about reflexivity: in reflecting upon past practice and incorporating theory, the social worker anticipates future work and adjusts their actions accordingly (Argyris and Schön 1974; Schön 1983). While this model is helpful to social work students on placement, for example, because it brings together the university-based learning with the spontaneous world of organisational-based practice (Dunk-West 2013, p. 113), is it true to say that reflexivity ought to be central to a social workers' practice throughout their career?

It is useful to consider this reflexive action in relation to the claims about late modernity and the project of selfhood (Giddens 1991) discussed earlier in this chapter. One interpretation is that the emergence of social work as a profession coincided with the emergence of 'self as project'. In this way, the social work profession or social work self is another example of how broader forces have shaped a particular identity. In this sense, it is important to critically examine another model of reflexivity and this is where Mead's scholarship is useful. In understanding reflexivity as embedded in processes which produce identity, the role of reflexivity can be reconceptualised in a social work which has an understanding of its own identity as well as providing a way of thinking about the self which is helpful to educators and practitioners alike (Dunk-West 2013).

For Mead, reflexivity draws the self into the present: this is the point at which reflection takes place and is the point at which social interaction is embedded (Mead 1929). If we follow Mead's understanding of self-constitution, reflexivity is important in that it helps us understand the ways in which our selves are storied to others – for example, the 'I' and the 'me' as a social worker. There are two points at which Mead's theory of self translates to the emergence of one's social work self: firstly, in studies, social work students use play and games to interact while assuming the role of the social worker. Just as children learn about the world around them through such play and games (Mead 1925), so too do social work students learn to understand and internalise the values and ethics and appropriate ways to interact as a social worker. Secondly, it is a mistake to disembed reflexivity from the process of sociality: locating the identity of the social worker within social relations is vital. Mead tells us:

The self-conscious, actual self in social intercourse is the objective "me" or "me's" with the process of response continually going on and implying a fictitious "I" always out of sight of himself. Inner consciousness is socially organized by the importation of the social organization of the outer world. (Mead 1912, p. 57)

Interactionism, Selfhood and Reflexivity

Both Giddens and Mead highlight the importance of the social setting from the onset of human life (Adams 2003, p. 232), and Mead's idea of self is neither postmodern nor psychoanalytic (Jackson 2007, p. 7). Mead argues that reflexivity enables one to be an 'other' to oneself and this occurs through continual interaction with social processes (Mead 1913; Mead 1925). As noted above, it is also important to understand Mead's theory of learning in childhood since it fulfills an important function in the ongoing production of selfhood through sociality (Mead 1933).

Perhaps one of the most prominent areas of social work practice which has clearly adapted a psychological model of selfhood is in the area of children. Childhood has been unproblematically associated as a time when events which occur influence outcomes, experiences and relationships in later life. Recent interest in neuro-imaging, for example, in which childhood trauma is mapped and evidenced through brain scans is important to consider alongside a critical appreciation of what such knowledge brings to the work. The scientific community herald such developments in technology as allowing 'irrefutable evidence of the structural and functional changes that occur within the brains of these children' (Delima and Vimpani 2011, p. 43):

Since the advent of more complex imaging tools from the 1990s onwards... scientific evidence on maltreatment-induced brain injury has rapidly accelerated, such that it now permits identification of more subtle injuries. (Beers and De Bellis 2002; MacMillan et al. 2009)

Each of the studied areas within injured brains has demonstrated significant behavioural and cognitive developmental deficits in maltreated children, and the implications this has for the ecosystems within which the child develops and interacts. (Beers and De Bellis 2002; Bremner et al. 1999; De Bellis 2005; De Bellis, Broussard et al. 2001; Delima and Vimpani 2011)

Although this kind of knowledge acquisition can help to bring to the fore the impacts and implications of child maltreatment, neglect and trauma, it is important that technology does not supersede other forms of knowledge. What is evident in scientific research into trauma is that it reinforces the idea that biology is the primary source of knowledge, with other systems such as the social environment of the individual, seen as secondary. Here we see evidence of the prevalence of a scientific model of selfhood. It is as though the physical evidence of trauma is somehow more convincing than a personal narrative. Let us examine Mead's conceptualisation of childhood, since it differs from the dominant model used in social work.

For Mead, one of the central tasks in childhood is to learn about relating to others. This knowledge prepares individuals for interactions in future life. Through taking the role of others, such as 'acting as a parent' (Mead 1925, p. 80) and so on, '…the child is continually exciting in himself [sic] the responses to his own social acts' (Mead 1925, p. 81). In undertaking this kind of play, the child learns to view the world through the lens of the parent. Similarly, children take on the roles of those around them and through play they begin to anticipate the ways in which others engage in the world around them (Mead 1925, p. 81). Using their skills in imitation, children engage in game playing. Games are structured: there are clear rules which govern roles and behaviour (Mead 1925, p. 81). For Mead, games are important because the player must anticipate the views and responses of *all the participants*. Mead's 'generalized other' relates to the ability to anticipate others' behaviours and responses or the 'attitude of the community' (Mead 1934, p. 154). This routine skill (Crossley 2001, p. 145) is central to social interaction since intuitive knowledge of broader society's values and attitudes enables actors to successfully engage in social interactions. Cognitive processes are only relevant in so much as they mediate the social environment. Mead says:

> We can talk to ourselves, and this we do in the inner forum of what we call thought. We are in possession of selves just insofar as we can and do take the attitudes of others toward ourselves and respond to those attitudes. We approve of ourselves and condemn ourselves. We pat ourselves upon the back and in blind fury attack ourselves…In this fashion, I conceive, have selves arisen in human behavior [sic] and with the selves their minds. (Mead 1925, p. 83)

Thus cognitive processes or 'internal conversations' (Mead 1925) are a manifestation of social experiences:

> The growth of the self arises out of a partial disintegration – the appearance of the different interest in the forum of reflection, the reconstruction of the social world, and the consequent appearance of the new self that answers to the new object. (Mead 1913, p. 62)

Mead argues that reflexivity is needed for social functioning (Jackson 2007, p. 8). As we noted earlier in this chapter, he argues that what people think of as their 'minds' are, in fact, firmly locatable outside their selves (in contrast to psychoanalytic notions of subjectivity which see identity as related to an 'inner' world of individual thoughts and reflections): minds therefore 'arise' only through social interactions (Mead 1913). Mead argues that 'reflectiveness, then, is the essential condition, within the social process, for the development of mind' (1934, p. 134).

The notion of reflexivity is therefore a compulsory condition for sociality, which in turn 'makes' the self. It is a feature of human life and human action (Archer 2007). Gagnon says:

> Being reflexive is enormously complex because the actor has to think of many possibilities and many consequences not only for others, but for the constitution of the self. The pressure to select, to choose one of the many lines of action, increases the more you get into the public world, but at the same time the integrity of the fantasy must be maintained…The task of the actor is to continually link and adjust and transform and stabilize the interpersonal and the cultural while maintaining the plausibility of the self. (Gagnon 2011, in Gagnon and Simon 2011 [1973], p. 315)

In social work, our notion of identity is manifest in our practice but is also suggested in the ways in which we conceptualise reflexivity as vital to social work practice (Fook 1999). For example, routinely compartmentalised and often routine to everyday practice, it is the ways in which social workers assess that is problematic at best (Dunk-West 2011) and dangerous at worst (Laming 2003). Coded through medical discourses, social work assessments require the author to compartmentalise the self as though life can easily be fit into such boxes. Social work scholarship has marginally engaged in its own deliberations about developing a social work self which has underplayed the role of a critique of 'reflexive' scholars in social work.

Here George Herbert Mead's scholarship is useful. His depiction of reflexivity as embedded in processes out of which the self emerges is helpful. Social work students learn how to integrate theory and practice through deliberately slowing down the movement of their practice through taking time to reflect, breaking down previous action and discussing their practice in detail through the process of supervision (see, for example, Cleak and Wilson 2004; Wilson 2000). Yet when social workers graduate, they often speed up their practice by shedding the reflexive deliberations so integral to their social work education. Just as with Mead's social interaction becoming 'routinized' (Mead 1913; 1934), so too can social workers' practices be seen as being routinised. Routinisation pushes reflexivity back into the social act: reflexivity is a requirement of sociality (Mead

1913), however, it is not, in and of itself, significant. This adoption of Mead's theory of selfhood has implications for social work however before considering what sociological social work entails in relation to the social work self, we now move on to consider power in the role of self-formation in social work.

Mead and Foucault

Power is important to considering not only our own conception of ourselves as professionals, but in thinking more broadly about society and inequalities. At the beginning of the chapter we outlined some of the stereotypes and negative media portrayals which exist. Social work has had a long history in addressing social inequalities which was examined throughout Chapter 1 of this book. Thinking about social work and the ways in which it is portrayed involves understanding the profession from the 'outside'.

Mead's theory of self can sit alongside other scholarship. For example, the social constructionism of Berger and Luckmann (Berger and Luckmann 1967) fits well with Mead's prominent role of sociality in generating the self. Mead can also be united with other theorists from other traditions (Burkitt 1994). Perhaps a surprising partnership is Mead and Foucault since their respective treatment of the individual and society markedly differ. Yet there are points of convergence and synergy, and Foucault brings an analysis of power which is helpful when thinking about selfhood (Dunk-West forthcoming).

Foucault examines society, including social institutions, practices and contexts through historical analysis (Macey 2009; Foucault 1972 [1969]). Understanding social and cultural practices using the historical perspective draws away from an individualised focus into one in which broader social patterns can be analysed. This process uproots the assumed dimensions to the concept of the individual. As Burkitt notes:

> First, the philosophical image of the self-contained individual…has been challenged by the focus on the social construction of self; and second, the notion of the possessive individual, so central to capitalism, has been critiqued by the idea that the self is a cultural and historical creation. (Burkitt 1994, p. 7)

In this way it becomes easier to critically understand selfhood but also to contextualise the social shifts occurring in tandem with self-production. The interest in identity or selfhood is an interest which is generated due to the convergence of particular social practices, shifts and institutions.

The concept of social work itself ought to be understood alongside socio-cultural and historical forces. Combining Foucault's theories of self and power with a critical tradition, for example Marxism, can help better theorise power and selfhood in social work:

> If we argue that power is widely diffused through networks of social relations, does it dissolve the critical theorist's claim that dominant groups possess power over subordinate groups? I do not believe it does. To acknowledge that power is diffused does not mean that people's powers are equal. Although Foucault's analysis of power undermines earlier critical analyses of society as a monolithic power structure, his theory is compatible with many critical perspectives...He is concerned with the ways in which these global manifestations of power are influenced by decentralized and localized forms of power. (Pease 2002, p. 139)

Foucauldian theories of power place it with forces outside the individual. This is quite a radical idea in social work because the profession's traditional placement of power is at the individual level. The notion of 'empowerment', for example, is reliant upon a conceptualisation of a self which is capable of internalising power and 'holding' it there. The idea of self-esteem, for example, involves the idea that an individual builds confidence in themselves in order to become resilient against criticism or oppression. It is important to note that self-esteem is a part of a broader theory of self which draws from psychoanalytic theory and the subsequent therapy culture which pervades much of late modern society in advanced capitalist nations (Furedi 2004).

Identity is a relatively under-theorised concept in social work (Dunk-West 2012). This is surprising on one level, given the centrality of human interaction in the profession. In sociology there is much theorising about selfhood, particularly in recent times. Some of the literature about identity or selfhood which comes from sociology draws from a range of disciplines including developmental psychology and philosophy, which is perhaps a point of overlap for social work given social work's reliance upon developmental psychology for its conceptions of identity.

A theory of identity is discernible from the very first meeting between a social worker and their client(s). The ways in which social workers think about themselves as professionals and the ways in which they categorise and make sense of their clients' lives draw from theories of selfhood. However these theories of selfhood are only able to be articulated or understood if there are alternative ways to think. Sociological social work involves understanding theories of selfhood and identity in relation to key historical events. This type of work entails researching and thinking about oneself and the world in which the self is immersed.

This chapter has examined social work identity in terms of the wider profession as well as social workers' personal identities and their ongoing construction. We have explored George Herbert Mead's theory of self as emergent from social interaction and argued that this theory of self has much to offer social work. We have explored how this kind of knowledge about the self differs from existing traditions utilised in social work such as the ways in which childhood is conveyed through medicalised and scientific discourses. We have argued that sociological social work entails a deeper engagement with theories of selfhood and a broader understanding of how theories of self alter social workers' responses to the people with whom they work. In the next chapter we move on to consider how social workers' identities are realised in the context of their organisational setting.

Recommended Reading

Castells, M. (1997) *The Power of Identity*, Massachusetts, USA: Blackwell Publishers Inc.

Dunk-West, P. (2013) *How to be a Social Worker: A Critical Guide for Students*, Basingstoke: Palgrave Macmillan.

Mead, G.H. (1913) The Social Self, in *G.H. Mead: A Reader*, edited by Silva, F.C., Abingdon: Routledge.

Chapter 4
Social Work Identity and Bureaucracy

Introduction

Organisations are the location of most social work practice and have an impact on the 'structure and structuring' of social work identity, to use a theoretical concept in the rich work of the sociologist Bourdieu, and one that is introduced more fully in this chapter. Social workers will work within organisational requirements, collaborate in networks with other organisations, use individually their agency and persuasive abilities to advocate for organisational change, be part of the organisational culture, and at a personal level spend days, months, years, sometimes whole careers within them. The exercise of personal labour, ingenuity, resilience, emotional engagement and, if in paid work, the gaining of remuneration, are all in the mix. The efficacy of social work heavily relies on the social worker's analytical sensibilities, or what Bauman and May (2001) describe as abilities to search, discover and understand as an ongoing project.

Organisations occupy an important social space in social work practice (Jones and May 1992) and they are 'a space of relations which are just as real as a geographic space' (Bourdieu 2002, p. 124). These organisational fields of practice are not the sole structuring factor of the social work role. The social worker has a reference point in the constellation of a global social work, in relations with the people for whom social workers work, and in their own personal and social work identities. These reference points are not static or fixed and neither is the knowledge we come to understand. Social workers also have multiple accountabilities, and in their work they balance and reconcile these tensions, including the different views on what it is they do and the reasons for doing it (Ife 1997).

It might be assumed that in advanced industrialised countries the organisations that employ social workers have more in common than different characteristics and that this is because they share a broad mission to respond to 'human needs and problems' (Hasenfeld and English 1974, p. 3). This is not so. They will vary on every possible dimension. A recent Australian Productivity Report on the Not-for-profit (NFP) sector mapped the Australian NFP sector using the dimensions of purpose, activities and outcomes, organisational structure, legal status, market status, and financing sources (2010, p. 7). The

Table 4.1   **Activities usually included within the not-for-profit sector: International Classification of Non-Profit Organisations (ICNPO)**

Activity	Includes
Culture & Recreation	Media & communications; Visual arts, architecture, ceramic art; Performing arts; Historical, literary & humanistic societies; Museums; Zoos & aquariums; Sports; Recreation & social clubs; Service clubs.
Education & Research	Elementary, primary & secondary education; Higher education; Vocational/technical schools; Adult/continuing education; Medical research; Science & technology; Social sciences, policy studies.
Health	Hospitals & rehabilitation; Nursing homes; Mental health & crisis intervention; Other health services (for example, public health & wellness education).
Social Services	Child welfare, child services & day care; Youth services & youth welfare; Family services; Services for the handicapped; Services for the elderly; Self-help & other personal social services; Disaster/emergency prevention & control; Temporary shelters; Refugee assistance; Income support & maintenance; Material assistance.
Environment	Pollution abatement & control; Natural resources conservation & protection; Environmental beautification & open spaces; Animal protection & welfare; Wildlife preservation & protection; Veterinary services.
Development & Housing	Community & neighbourhood organisations; Economic development; Social development; Housing associations & assistance; Job training programs; Vocational counselling & guidance; Vocational rehabilitation & sheltered workshops.
Law, Advocacy & Politics	Advocacy organisations; Civil rights associations; Ethnic associations; Civic associations; Legal services; Crime prevention & public policy; Rehabilitation of offenders; Victim support; Consumer protection associations; Political parties & organisations.
Philanthropic intermediaries & voluntarism promotion	Grant-making foundations; Volunteerism promotion & support; Fund-raising organisations.

International	Exchange/friendship/cultural programs; Development assistance associations; International disaster and relief organisations; International human rights and peace organisations.
Religion	Congregations (including churches, synagogues, mosques, shrines, monasteries & seminaries); Associations of congregations.
Business & Professional Associations & Unions	Business associations (organisations that work to promote, regulate & safeguard the interests of special branches of business); Professional associations (organisations promoting, regulating & protecting professional interests); Labour unions.
Not elsewhere classified	All other non-profit organisations including cooperative schemes, manufacturers, wholesalers, retailers, cemetery operators.

Source: Reproduction of Table 1, Activities usually included within the not-for-profit sector, *Contribution of the Not-for-Profit Sector*, p. XXVII, Productivity Commission)

diversity revealed was remarkable. One dimension in which NFP organisations differed was in functional area, as shown in the table above from the Australian Productivity Report.

A similar differentiated pattern is found in other OECD countries and as noted by the World Bank the NFP sector has 'mushroomed' in recent times (http://web.worldbank.org/). This analysis has wider relevance beyond the not-for-profit sector. It signals the breadth of workplace experiences that social workers may have and potential isolation as a result of such diversification. It also means social workers need to think about and know the context in which they are stepping into; they will be different. Given this diversity, social workers' experiences of their work will be affected by the idiosyncratic nature of the context within which they work. This can make it difficult to draw together common goals or feel a sense of shared occupational space. There is landscape of heterogeneous organisations and where they receive a majority of their funds from governments, they will share compliance conditions and practices reflecting neo-liberal social policy (Gillingham 2007; Carson and Kerr 2010).

This chapter examines the setting and context in which social work takes place, contexts that have paradoxically become increasingly complex and standardised. The sociological ideas of Max Weber and Pierre Bourdieu are introduced.

Who Employs Social Workers?

Organisations that employ social workers will range in size from large to small organisations, both as measured by numbers of paid and unpaid workers and in financial terms. They could be a government agency with a prescribed mandate, a non-government agency funded through a governmental contractual arrangement or by independent sources or a private provider. The values, goals and missions of organisations will be diverse. Organisations might be part of larger regional or national networks, or a sole service delivery agency and these structural arrangements will have implications for the extent that services and programs are locally determined. The representation of, and relationships with, the people for whom the organisation exists will vary, as will the social work role. For example, if there is a contract from government to deliver employment services this will shape the remit of the service or program delivery, and therefore what the social worker does, and the client identity and relations with the organisations (Ife 1997).

Social work employing organisations could have long histories stretching back to a time before the origins of the post-Second World War welfare state, and this history will be part of the culture and woodwork. Or they could be a creature of more current times and dominant welfare service discourses. An example of the former is the Australian Red Cross which was formed in 1914, incorporated in 1941 and now each Australian state and territory provides a range of community, health services and humanitarian assistance. In contrast Ingeus Programs[1] is a more recent service company founded by Therese Rein and a colleague in 1989 to provide employment services and with a revenue stream from funding by government outsourced contracts. Ingeus is an international provider with services in the UK, across Europe, Australia and throughout Asia.

This landscape has implications for the intellectual tools of the social worker to notice, make sense and understand patterns in the competing discourses, politics and agendas within organisations. One human response to how neo-liberal practices may be changing organisational life is to blame management who are implementing policies and practices. Compton and Galaway (1979, p. 483) note:

> ...it will not help the worker, or the client for the worker to see the bureaucracy as something bad that should be condemned at every turn. Rather, it must be understood as a reality – a complex system in which both the worker and client are sub-systems. Given this important fact of life – we need to learn to work

---

1 http://www.ingeus.com.au/pages/home/0/home.html.

within and to change bureaucracy rather than to simply make ourselves feel good by holding bureaucracy as bad. (Pruger 1978)

What analytical concepts do social workers use to think about what the organisation is requiring them to do, and how do they interpret and navigate the tensions between organisational remit and social work role and the emotions this will generate? Related is: how do social workers act with positive agency in their organisational context, and in the interests of the people with whom they work, in fulfilment of their social work purpose, and their own self-fulfilment? It is these questions that we focus on in this chapter. These are not new questions by any means but they are most surely complex. The paradoxes and dilemmas faced by social workers in organisational settings have long preoccupied social workers and social work writers (Bartlett 1970; Jones and May 1992; Ife 1997; Dominelli 1997). However, given the nature of change in contemporary life and the social order that we sketch out in Chapter 1, the dilemmas spelt out above are especially acute (Hyslop 2012).

Neo-liberal ideas and values shape organisations more than they have done before, even though these ideas are resisted and will not be the totality of discourses and organisational practices (Ife 1997; Clarke 2004b); time is pressured and there is much to be done; digital technology enables work to happen outside the organisational buildings and supposed 'office hours' and all is speeding up (Lemert 2007) themes we take up in Chapters 8 and 9 of this book. Demands on services are also growing (ACOSS 2011) which places additional pressures on social workers within services.

Critical and reflexive thinking is a necessary tool for the social worker, not only to support them, understand the contexts in which they practice (Jones and May 1992; Ife 1997) and see the openings to voice alternative ideas, but so they are not deafened in the loudness of the dominant neo-liberal discourse and so that hope and social justice imagination is not extinguished. Social work's relatively recent inclusion of Bourdieu's work is identified as providing an excellent framework to better understand and question the relationship of the social worker in her/his organisational setting – and the subsequent identity created through the symbiosis of the social worker's habitus within their field. Bourdieu's critics in social work (Garrett 2007) highlight the limits of his theories (for example, for not accounting appropriately for agency or cultural matters) yet we suggest his notions of habitus and field provide an enduring and relevant model for social work students to better understand, and integrate, their practice learning with their emerging professional self. To examine these issues in more detail the example of risk management is used in the chapter.

Thinking About Organisations

Organisations can be analysed in many ways: through a prism of authority structure and control; human relations and organisational behaviour; by formal functions, as a unit in systems interfacing with a wider environment and through the prism of decision making analysis (Silverman 1970; Couldshed and Mullender 2001). From these different entry points into thinking about organisations have come various theories: classic organisational theories of rational/legal bureaucracy (Weber 1947); scientific management, with a focus on techniques for efficiency in production (Taylor 1913); organisations as adaptive social units (Selznick 1948) and human relations theories (Mayo 1945) which have focused on the human need for satisfaction and fulfilment in their work. Over time new ideas have built on the legacies of these seminal theories, for instance in the work of complex organisational theorists like Etzioni (1980) and Perrow (1986), the new managerialism which has extended Taylor's ideas of scientific management (Considene and Painter 1997), and new emerging organisational analysis that employs the theoretical lens of Bourdieu.

Max Weber

A classical theoretical approach to a study of organisational life is the work of the German sociologist Max Weber who was thinking and writing in the later part of the nineteenth century and early twentieth century. In his work *The Theory of Social and Economic Organisation* he systematically analysed and laid out ideal types of authority and power in relation to social order. Couldshed and Mullender (2001, p. 28) describe that Weber was '...interested in what makes people follow instructions'. Weber provides ways to think about 'legitimate authority' and identified pure or ideal types as conceptual tools, or abstract ways to think about authority. Rational authority he describes as '...resting on a belief in the "legality" of patterns of normative rules and the right of those elevated to authority under such rules to issues commands (legal authority)' (Weber 1964, p. 328).

Weber identified the rational bureaucracy to be a dominant social unit formed within and expanding in industrialisation (Nisbet 1970). Nisbet writes:

> Bureaucracy falls...within Weber's category of rational domination; it is the mode of hierarchy that supplants patrimonial, charismatic, and/or traditional authority. (1970, p. 145)

Weber categories the key aspects in rational/legal bureaucratic structures: responsibilities or duties of the organisational members are precise; there is a hierarchal structure that aligns with roles and responsibilities; people who hold and exercise power do so because of the organisational roles they occupy, not their personal attributes or because they hold traditional power; there is a separation of personal ties and obligations from workings of the organisation; the employment of skilled people for the jobs as required, that is 'they are appointed not anointed' and there is separation in the ownership of the means of production (Weber 1964, p. 330–32). Weber identified that the rational bureaucratic organisation is best able to deliver outcomes efficiently under the conditions of industrial capitalism. As Lippmann and Aldrich write for Weber, 'The power of tradition gave way to the power of standard' (2001, p. 4).

Weber introduced a powerful and enduring metaphor for the rational/legal bureaucracy and how it worked on the human spirit. This was the metaphor of the rational/legal bureaucracy as an 'iron cage'. This image evokes the sense of deadening restrictions on the person within the organisation. Weber writes in *The Protestant Ethic and the Spirit of Capitalism* (1958):

> No one knows who will live in this cage in the future, or whether at the end of this tremendous development [of disenchantment] entirely new prophets will arise, or there will be a great rebirth of old ideas, or, if neither, mechanized petrifaction...For of the last stage of this cultural development, it might truly be said: "Specialists without spirit, sensualists without heart". (1958, p. 182)

Max Weber's insights about power and authority and the iron cage of rational bureaucracy can assist social workers in thinking about matters like aspects of the increasing tightly controlled workplaces in which they practice. Clegg and Baumeler capture this challenge: 'Modern organisational forms are not likely to be replaced, overcome or defeated but their solidity can be eroded by changing liquidity, weakening their structures, penetrating them with new forms of social relations' (Clegg and Baumeler 2010, p. 1718). One of the challenges for social workers given the organisational and policy contexts in which they work, and the pressures in organisations is to avoid 'disenchantment' and to maintain a positive imagination for how organisations might be and how the social worker can practice in ways that are congruent with the principles and values of social work.

Organisational Actors: Habitus and Field

Bourdieu's (Bourdieu and Wacquant 1992) work on habitus and field is a way into thinking about the complicated workings of organisations and the underlying structures, relations and possibilities that may not be readily apparent. His work in this area is extensive and what follows is but some salient points for this discussion of social work, organisations and sociological social work. Bourdieu's constructs of 'habitus' and 'field' depict the dynamic influences of interactions between humans and social structures. Habitus is defined as:

> ...cognitive structures which social agents implement in their practical knowledge of the social world...[and] are internalised, embodied social structures. (Bourdieu 1984, p. 468)

Essentially this is a script pattern or 'systems of durable, transposable dispositions' (Bourdieu 1977, p. 72) formed in and through the social world into which a person is raised and socialised. This socialisation process gives structure to how a person mentally interprets the world, takes action in the world and interprets what they do and experience. This is an internalised social structure that structures thinking or provides 'schemes of perception' and is reflected in the body. Sallaz writes of this as an 'Embodied *sens* of reality through which social agents perceive and act on the world' (2010, p. 296).

History is indelibly present in habitus. Bourdieu writes:

> Habitus is not the fate that some people read into it. Being the product of history, it is an *open system of dispositions* that is constantly subjected to experiences, and therefore constantly affected by them in way that reinforces or modifies its structure. It is durable but not eternal. (Bourdieu and Wacquant 1992, p. 133)

Habitus is in relation to field or what Bourdieu depicts to be 'a set of objective, historical relations between positions and anchored in certain forms of power (or capital)' (Bourdieu and Wacquant 1992, p. 16).

Bourdieu defines key aspects of a field as relationality as 'not interactions between agents or intersubjective ties between individuals but object relations which exist "independently of individual consciousness and will", as Marx said' (Bourdieu and Wacquant 1992, p. 97). These are social relations played out in 'social microcosms' (Bourdieu and Wacquant 1992, p. 97). Bourdieu gives examples of fields: the artistic field, religious field, economic field, journalistic field, fashion designer fields and field of cultural associations. Social work is a field and there will be fields within this field also called 'social spaces'. As Emirbayer and Williams (2005, p. 690) note these fields in a Bourdieaun sense are '...relatively autonomous social microcosms'.

Within a field are rules, power relations that can be defined as relations of domination and sub-ordination, and the expression or distribution and recognition of forms of capital (cultural, economic and social capital). Relations between 'people in the field defines the structure of the field' (Bourdieu and Wacquant 1992, p. 99) and thus consideration of the relationality between people in a field and what results is crucial. Furthermore fields can change. Bourdieu writes:

As a space of potential and active forces, the field is also a *field of struggles* aimed at preserving or transforming the configuration of these forces...The strategies of agents depend on their position in the field, that is, in the distribution of specific capital, and on the perception that they have of the field depending on the point of view they take *on* the field as a view taken from a point i*n* the field. (Bourdieu and Wacquant 1992, p. 101)

Whilst an organisation may itself denote a field, depending on its boundaries, as noted above there will be fields within an meta organisational field, and the humans who enter the organisation bring with them their own habitus. As Bourdieu notes '...the space of interaction is the locus where the intersection between several different fields is realised' (Bourdieu and Wacquant, p. 257). Fields are identified by coming to make known 'the taken for granted, unquestioned, spontaneous, and commonsensical understandings that prevail across space' (Emirbayer and Williams, 2005, p. 695).

Garrett (2007) argues that Bourdieu's work opens up thinking about how social structures interact with subjects and agency, about the power forces at work within fields, like social work, and the organisations that employ social work. In Bourdieu's frame of reference the interior spaces of the 'iron cages' are complicated, relational and spaces for different relations to be formed. Hallett notes:

When people enter organistions, they bring their habitus – and their relation to the broader social order – with them, and individual practices within an organisation are informed (but not determined) by the habitus (linked to a position in the social order). (2003, p. 130)

The social order referred to in the preceeding quote is important for understanding organisations and thinking about social work, and it is to this we now turn.

Neo-liberal Ascendency

Major changes in governmental discourses and policies, and the dynamics within organisations, result from the uptake of neo-liberal ideas and the concurrent extension of rationality in contemporary western societies. Writers such as Frederich Hayek, Milton and Rose Friedman, and in the Australian context Peter Saunders from the Centre for Independent Studies, have been powerful exponents of neo-liberal ideas, which have been influential in changing governmental practices. These arguments are rooted in individualist/ anti-collectivist discourses (Bryson 1992) and in general terms they argue that it is free markets which are the better mechanisms for meeting human needs, and for creating and supporting wellbeing for individuals and wellbeing at a societal level. In contrast to other perspectives these neo-liberal thinkers argue that overly generous welfare states are the source of dependency (on services and money from national and sub-national governments); they deplete an individual of motivation and the exercise of will, and their own abilities to be 'self-responsible', and expose people more to the controls and restrictions of government bureaucracy (summarised by Bessant et al. 2006, p. 43).

They argue ultimately it is these conditions, in combination, that diminish people's freedom and self-expression (Saunders 2002). Further to this, welfare states consume large amounts of taxpayer money and this undermines higher income earner incentives to earn and drags on investment and economic growth. Milton Friedman in the introduction to his book *Capitalism and Freedom*, from a North American perspective, writes:

> How can we benefit from the promise of government while avoiding the threat to freedom? Two broad principles embodied in our Constitution give an answer...First the scope of government must be limited. Its major function must be to protect our freedom from the enemies outside our gates and from fellow-citizens: to preserve law and order, to enforce private contracts, to foster competitive markets beyond this major function, government may enable us at times to accomplish jointly what we would find more difficult to accomplish severally. However the use of government in this way is fraught with danger... by relying on private enterprise, in both economic and other activities, we can insure that the private sector is a check on the power of the government sector and an effective protection of freedom of speech, of religion, and of thought. (1962, pp. 2–3)

Over the last 20 to 30 years OECD nations have taken up these neo-liberal ideas, and have introduced culturally specific variants of neo-liberal public policy. This uptake is what Fiona Williams terms '...the creation of the three Ms – markets, managers and mixed economies' (1999, p. 670). In practice the three Ms include supposedly downsized governments, although the evidence on this is fallacious, implementing measures like privatisation, outsourcing and contractualism as well as public administration reform.

In countries such as England and Australia, public administration is now firmly dominated by neo-liberal market values; efficiency indicators predominate, accountability and performance are measured in economic terms, and services have adopted market language and practices. The focus is a new form of technical rational managerialism, or new public management (Painter 1997). For example, people who use the services of the Australian national social security agency Centrelink are called 'customers'. A market model is predicated on impersonal transactions where there are goods and services exchanged by 'rational self-interested actors' (Muetzelfeldt 1994, p. 137). These changed practices also include a redirection to risk management where risks are no longer collective risks to be responded to by the state, but private matters and responsibilities, as O'Malley writes '…governed better by individuals and markets' (O'Malley 2004, p. 11).

The following extract from the *Australian Report on Government Services 2012* highlights this market-orientated focus in public administration as can be seen in the use of words such as 'delivery/provider', and 'purchase services'.

> Governments use a mix of methods to deliver services to the community, including:
> - delivering or providing the services directly (a 'delivery/provider' role)
> - funding external providers through grants or the purchase of services (a 'purchaser' role)
> - subsidising users (through vouchers or cash payments) to purchase services from external providers
> - imposing community service obligations on public and private providers
> - providing incentives to users and/or providers, such as reducing tax obligations in particular circumstances (known as 'tax expenditures').
>
> (1.4 *Australian Report on Government Services 2012*)

In the United Kingdom during the Thatcher and Major years of the 1980s and 1990s, key government utilities were privatised such as British rail and telecommunication services (Clarke 2004b). Privatisation of services in Australia has been extensive and includes the outsourcing of the provision of water, electricity, prison services, ambulance services, and construction services. Neo-liberal policy measures also have seen reforms to create artificial 'internal markets' within government departments, for example within health services using models like the separation of the funder from the purchaser and the provider. These have been extremely divisive social policies which in turn have produced unequal social and economic outcomes.

There are now many reports that illustrate the gulfs between rich and poor, and the spatial nature of this inequality, and we take up this theme in Chapter 10.

Contestation to Neo-Liberalist Values

Whilst neo-liberal ideas are now dominant they are intensely contested and opposed (Mendes 2003a). Clarke argues that 'Living in a neo-liberal world is not necessarily the same as being neo-liberal. Attention to the different sorts of living with, in and against neo-liberal domination is a necessary antidote to "big picture" projections of its universalism' (2004b, p. 102). There is strong critique of the neo-liberal position and this includes the voicing of counter positions from social workers and sociologists. This is an ongoing political project, what Bryson terms '...part of the ongoing struggle over the distribution of power and resources in the various advanced capitalist societies' (1992, p. 15).

Counter arguments to the neo-liberal view include a critique that the moral construction of welfare dependency in neo-liberalism is blunt, harsh, individualistic and simplistic (see, for example, Williams 1999, p. 676). We all are dependent in various forms, as Williams' articulates '...it is ironic that those who are claiming welfare are seen as dependent, no matter how engaged or responsible for others they may be, whilst those who are market dependent are seen as independent' (Williams 1999, p. 676). Earlier in this chapter we noted the term 'customer' as evidence of a consumer model of service provision. Similarly, we argue that it is not a coincidence that the term 'service user' has become so ubiquitous in social work in England. Although the term can be helpful in highlighting particular needs it 'others' people who use services as distinct from the rest of the community or population. The term 'service user' sets up the notion of 'the dependant' in neo-liberal individualist ideology because it implies that there are others who do not use services. We all use services, whether these come from health service sectors, educational service sectors or other organisations providing services.

Furthermore the neo-liberal view does not account for collective interventions in forms that are not noted, considered or debated by the public as 'welfare' (Bryson 1992). Richard Titmuss (1969) advocates this viewpoint in his work *Social Division of Welfare,* in which he cogently presents the case that 'collective interventions' are more than support to people on low incomes through social assistance. Collective intervention occurs as well through occupational welfare and fiscal welfare, that is, government support via the routes of the workplace and tax system. Superannuation or pension support is an example here. Titmuss also passionately argues for the dignity that universalism can allow, where there is the absence of stigma and prejudice. Alternatives to neo-liberalism come from communitarians who argue for a switch from the market to communities as an 'alternative to liberalism' (Etzioni 1996, p. 1) and that civil society is better placed to human needs and nourish social values.

Social Workers in the Crux of Change

Organisations that employ social workers sit in the crux of contested social policy. With the now pervasive practices of new public management, social workers have had to implement services or activities that they and their organisation may not support, and are against their habitus. The commitment within an organisation for community development, for example, may be withdrawn if the prevailing public policy direction and the money or contract to fund a service is for other types of interventions. This has been the case in many jurisdictions in Australia. Alternatively a new programme, for example about individualised health care may be introduced, again because this is the policy trend and what the service contracts dictate. In this sense creative social work may be a memory.

Further, there are compliance measures that need to be attended to and these take up much time. For example, reporting against performance indicators, purchasing certain amounts and types of insurance, undertaking quality service excellence, undergoing quality and standard accreditation, and adopting business plans and language (Alford and O'Neill 1994; Rose 1996; Domenilli 1997; Alessandrini 2010). Nyland and colleagues (2011) from Australian survey research estimated that not-for-profit organisations can spend up to as much as two months annually, in other words two months of downtime from what the organisation is meant do, meeting the requirements of government quality/ service excellence standards. The Australian Council of Social Service in their annual *Community Sector Survey for 2011* (ACOSS 2011, p. 76) report that increasing numbers of the organisations surveyed, and across all service types, have contract requirements that 'adversely affected their organisations ability to deliver services'. One of these compliance measures is risk management, a development that has consumed much organisational time and money.

Risk and Organisational Service Provision

Kemshall (2002) argued over a decade ago that risk is now a central 'organising logic' in public policy and social welfare provision and this has proven prophetic. Michael Powers, author of a book *The Risk Management of Everything* (2004, p. 9), chronicles how over the last two decades 'Risk management has invaded organisational life'. With the invasion has come a proliferation of risk concepts and metrics: 'populations at risk', 'risk factors', 'managing risk', risk management enterprise, risk management global standards such as IOS 3000, 'risk tolerance', 'risk appetite', 'risk decision making matrixes',' risk treatment plans' and with this an extremely profitable industry with a healthy risk appetite ready to develop products, guides, tools, and training to ensure organisations across all sectors of society – public, private and civil society – know how risk can be best managed.

Risk management can take many forms depending on variables such as organisational size (in revenue and staffing), bureaucratic form and governance and the extent to which the 'risk management invasion' has taken hold. Some organisations implement comprehensive organisational approaches so that risk management is intrinsic to decision making and service requirements. In this situation the rules, regulations and responsibilities of the workforce will be risk management driven, and from the top to the bottom of the organisation. Other organisations, perhaps because they are not as large or owing to their institutional architecture, may limit risk management to external outings or events, or adopt a tighter 'increased vigilance and avoidance' approach (Verity 2009).

Whichever form risk management takes, there will be very few social welfare services in developed countries as well as global organisations that remain untouched by the nomenclature and practice of risk. 'Risk assessment', 'populations at risk', 'risk factors', 'managing risk', and 'risk aversion' are common organisational terms. Driving this has been a normative acceptance that these practices are necessary, and evidence for this is given in examples of the damages and compensation awarded by the courts, and the need to keep children, workers, and consumers safe. Risk has also become individualised and related to occupational issues rather than addressing broader social inequalities. Recent research into the occupational practices of street-based sex workers found that individualised accounts of risk obscured physical and sexual violence towards this group of women. This research argues that risk ought to be recognised as socially embedded and should be understood through the ways in which the work is socially framed and reinforced through social norms and values (Leaker and Dunk-West 2011).

Verity (2005; 2009), from survey research in two time periods (2005 and 2008/2009), documented a spread of risk management in South Australian not-for-profit organisations who have steadily spent more time and resources in risk management. In both surveys NFP organisations report that they had stopped delivering some services because of risk management concerns. Most typically these were for services involved in direct work with children, youth related activities such as camps and outdoor activities, and sexual education programs. 25 per cent of the survey respondents in 2008/09 report that they had ceased or limited providing physical activity programs and facilities because of public liability concerns and risk management. Here are some of the accounts from participants:

> Risk has reduced our capacity to participate in community events, i.e. excursions, community visits. This in turn has limited our curriculum offered. (2009 respondent)

> We are cautious about certain programs and have to curb some effective activities. (2009 respondent)

> Events are far more costly as a result of the number of precautions we must now take – water, shade, additional staff ratios etc. This increase in insurance

premiums has given the centre less money to spend on other things like equipment to improve facilities. (2009 respondent)

It is a necessity but a pain. (2009 respondent)

These findings confirm the results of a not-for-profit risk survey conducted by an Australian and New Zealand private sector consultancy firm who write: '... it was interesting to note that 77 per cent of respondents would avoid the risk by doing such things as not proceeding with the activity if it was considered an appropriate action' (2010, p. 52). Organisations in Verity's studies stopped or cut back activities because of imagined future risks. But often this was because of a generalised anxiety and apprehension that the activity might one day be a negative risk (Verity 2008) not because there was firm evidence on the basis of calculations, for example, of injury claims. The study shows a small but not insignificant reporting of less community development and advocacy because it is seen as 'risky' in terms defined by prevailing risk management assessments. At one level the findings paint a picture of the risks to active participation and the 'we' of civil society if community groups, dance classes, organisation of fetes and fairs, advocates or protestors, curtail what they are doing or are very far away from what motivated them to come together, because of the impacts of risk management and insurance. What of being able to take risks and challenge existing power relations in the pursuit of goals of social justice, meeting human needs and supporting 'stronger communities'?

The study also shows that an unfettered risk culture is being challenged. Many respondents question the basis by which risks for community sector organisations are defined. As Verity writes, 'They question the relationship of a claims history (especially when it is low) to establishing risks and pricing the premium, and the underlying value basis, assumptions and knowledge used by insurers to construct certain activities as 'risky' and therefore more costly to insure, if indeed able to be insured at all. For example, by whose values and on what knowledge basis is youth sexuality education a risk?' (Verity 2005 p. 31).

Bourdieu argues that habitus shapes our dispositions, which has a bearing on imagination, which brings us back to risk management. Risk practices within organisations establish reference points for decision-making, resource allocation patterns and therefore the construction of 'futures'. Risk management is based firmly in imagination but the use of imagination involves thinking about what might go wrong. Ulrich Beck calls this the 'attempt to anticipate the worst possible turn' (2007, p. 129) type of risk management. He (1992; 1999b) explains this through a theory about 'risk society', a social world that is the upshot of complex and dynamic processes where modernist industrial era institutions have bent back onto themselves, inducing in the reflex new risks and fears of risk. In a risk society, emerging scientific frontiers (for example, the human genome), information technologies and associated global communications, within and beyond nation state social transformations, generate and transfer risks, but they also contribute to heightened knowledge and awareness of the risks we 'might face'. On this latter point Beck vividly paints a case where individual and collective risk awareness, through mental processes of imagining what may go wrong in the future, give way to more anxiety and fear, and with this a sense of responsibility to do something with this knowledge. This, in turn, generates more measures to ensure these risks do not eventuate, and so on and so on. The seeds of a normative risk culture flower. A respondent in Verity's 2008/09 study comments about risk:

> It has become a mantra which has a life of its own. My job is in middle management, and I adapt fairly easily to the change in climate, but I cannot help feeling that the community has been the loser. People even say the words "liability" as an excuse for anything, even if it is not something which would stand up. And so community attitudes change we start to tolerate restrictions which are inhuman almost. (e.g. The women who had been, for many years, making cakes and biscuits for the residents of the local nursing home and having morning tea with them, being prevented from continuing because of the "public risk"). We have become quite poor about assessing the risk of losing some very reliable aspects of our community by going down the path we have. (2009 respondent)

What we need is a way to think about organisations in which critical perspectives provide an antidote to temper overzealous approaches to risk and the impacts of other neo-liberal infused practices. Such a perspective involves understanding the experiences at a personal level within organisations, wider organisational practices and a view of the dynamics located in wider societal dynamics. Developments like risk management discussed earlier can be seen as forces strengthening the bars of the iron cage. Perhaps more aptly it could be said that the walls of the iron cage are closing in.

In this chapter we have explored some of the complexities involved in the organisational context and broader neo-liberal policy context within which social workers are placed. There are many practice dilemmas generated by deepening neo-liberal welfare state social policies and service and organisational changes; service demands constricting room to move in practice, and personal matters for the workers in both thinking about and responding in their work.

The challenges generate questions about the efficacy of available theoretically-informed practice models as intellectual maps or compasses for practice in complex situations. Furthermore, given the diversity of the sectors that employ social workers, how to share knowledge of practice approaches without slipping into a franchise mentality that may squash a worker's own critical and responsive abilities?; qualities especially necessary given the various experiences of social relations and economic conditions across geographic areas.

Sociological concepts about organisational power and rationality and the metaphor of the 'iron cage' from Weber and of fields, capital and habitus from Bourdieu have useful transferability to the challenges of the social worker in a neo-liberal social context. They can assist the social work analysis that is needed about organisations and the power relations at work within them and support the social worker in their own work for the people they work for and the broader social work goal of social justice.

Further Reading

Bourdieu, P. and Wacquant, L. (1992) *An Invitation to Reflexive Sociology*, Chicago: University of Chicago Press.

Kemshall, H. (2002) *Risk, Social Policy and Welfare*, Buckingham: Open University Press.

Lupton, D. (1999) *Risk*, London: Routledge.

Part 2
Collective Identity, Self and Agency

Chapter 5
Everyday Ethics: Developing Social Work Identity

In our contemporary world, events and conditions external to the individual have been interpreted through individualised discourses, giving rise to new dilemmas and struggles in everyday life. Topical social issues such as environmental change and sustainability, for example, filter down into personal dilemmas when the individual considers the extent to which these issues are relevant to them. The question of personal agency is central to this condition. In this chapter we consider ethics in light of the connection between the personal, everyday experience of the individual and the shifts in late modern life.

We argue that social workers must adopt a particular stance or preferred ethical framework in the context of the situation, but that this must also be congruent with their world-view and conduct in their everyday lives. Sociological social work in the area of ethics involves adopting 'the everyday' level of analysis and reflexive engagement with personal and social values, attitudes and awareness about responsibilities towards others. This chapter commences by critically examining ethics in social work and allied professions.

Everyday Ethics in Contemporary Society

Studies in the day-to-day practices of others help to frame action and behaviour in a way that enables a new level of understanding to emerge. Henri Lefebvre is the foremost scholar associated with 'the everyday' tradition (Gardiner 2004, p. 429) and he argues that:

> Everyday life is profoundly related to all activities, and encompasses them with all their differences and their conflicts; it is their meeting place, their bond and their common ground. It is in everyday life that the sum total of relations that make the human – and in every human being – a whole takes its shape and form. (Lefebvre 1991, p. 97)

The everyday is a useful tool in social work education (Dunk 2007; Dunk-West 2011) and in relation to ethics it helps to connect the life worlds of students and practitioners with the broader aspirations of the profession (Dunk-West 2013).

The connection between the everyday and ethics is evidenced in contemporary ethical viewpoints. For example, Peter Singer argues that the decision to purchase a particular consumer item limits the ability of the purchaser to spend that money on helping others: the ability to give is evident in everyday transactions (Singer 2009). In Singer's work, he highlights that now, more so than ever, people ought to consider themselves in the global context: this involves taking responsibility for the inequalities in resource distribution and making individual decisions to counter privilege through actions such as financial donations.

The individualisation thesis argues that the lifting of tradition has resulted in unprecedented levels of choice in our day-to-day lives (Beck 1994; Giddens 1991). Alongside increasing self-reflexivity, this may, in some part, account for the increasing engagement with choice in the consumer, personal and cultural spheres. Ferguson summarises this process:

> Constructing the self in a post-traditional order is a reflexive project in the sense that critical reflection and incoming information are constantly used by people to constitute and (re)negotiate their identities. While traditional "authorities", faith related and other, may still have an influence in some people's biographical projects, in reflexive modernity it is from experts, global media, books and so on that people draw information in reflexively making their lives. (Ferguson 2001, p. 45)

Although the reflexivity thesis has been contested, in particular for example, that opportunities to be reflexive are influenced on the grounds of class and gender (Skeggs 2004; Adkins 2003; 2002), it can be argued that in recent times there has been a conscious turn towards the ethical implications of everyday life. Ethical reflexivity involves negotiating day-to-day life whereby actors' transactions are deliberated upon and evaluated against a moral code. Crucially, ethical reflexivity needs to be considered in the same way that general assumptions about reflexivity ought to be made: that is, with full analysis of the conditions which limit reflexivity (Skeggs 2004; Adkins 2003; 2002).

Technology has played a role in this process through connecting people in new ways to work towards shared ethical action across an international context. Social media sites provide increased opportunities for individuals to showcase particular ethical practices and for individuals to reflexively engage with such information. Technology also enables ethical issues associated with everyday life to emerge. The recent call for CCTV in abattoirs, for example, is a movement which aims to make people more responsible for animal welfare by highlighting the reality of practices which occur in environments which are usually bracketed off from people's meat consumption. Although it is a stretch to argue that we 'see' the world in light of increased awareness of injustice, inequality and oppression, we argue that ethics in social work requires a micro sociological lens. Understanding social work ethics from a sociological perspective involves the acknowledgement of the everyday self in the production of the professional self: each is interrelated. A global perspective helps to frame the shifting ethical issues which emerge from our contemporary world. Together these lenses offer greater opportunities to theorise, research and practice in new ways.

Traditional Ethical Approaches in Social Work

There is a clear tradition in social work in which ethical approaches are outlined and their implications for practice elucidated (Banks 2003). Specifically, in social work, ethical approaches present themselves as resources to help make sense of the work. Just as the work is unique to the clients and social worker(s) involved, the ethical perspectives used are idiosyncratic to the worker and dependent upon the context in which the work takes place.

Some of the key ethical perspectives used in contemporary social work education include utilitarianism, Kantianism, virtue-based ethics and care ethics (Dunk-West 2013, p. 97–100). Each of these approaches is grounded in a theoretical or empirical framework. Another emerging strand in social work is the bioethical approach which, as its name suggests, is associated with medical professions.

Bioethical principles encourage professionals in avoiding harm, doing 'good' deeds, promoting people's autonomy and acting to promote justice (Beauchamp and Childress 1989). Bioethical approaches also promote truth-telling, confidentiality and being true to one's professional commitments (Beauchamp and Childress 1989).

At first glance, bioethics offers a simple and clearly articulated framework in which professional interactions take place. Despite the applicability to social work practice, some of the assumptions implicit to this approach require a sociological lens. Whereas rational-based frameworks can help decision making, the complexities are difficult to quantify. For example, informed consent as a rational choice in client decisions about the services and care they receive does little to account for the complex and specialist realm (Corrigan 2003) in which the emotive, social and biographical experiences converge.

Similarly, health professionals take self-determination into account in their work with clients and social workers place this value at the forefront of their practice. Self-determination is somehow very important to social work. A recent study, for example, found that final year social work students used the concept as a 'primary principle' compared to nursing students who placed it alongside a duty to care (Yeung et al. 2010, p. 1574). From the perspective of those receiving a service, self-determination as the expression of empowerment can have unintended consequences. Self-determination framed as a rational choice which promotes agency does little to account for the specialist knowledge of the professional nor the emotional dimension to decision-making, as articulated in the following account:

> When the highly paid specialist said the decision to have a fancy medical test was up to me, I knew "empowerment" had gone too far. I was paying him to make the decisions. But he was acting like the junior partner in my health care. I might have yelled "Power to the People" in some demo 20 years ago…but I didn't actually mean power to me over every technical decision that would crop up in my life. I didn't seek to be "empowered" in matters that bored me, like tax, or that totally baffled me, like expensive tests. I long for the old doctor-as-God, for the expert who would tell me what to do rather than lay out the odds. (Horin 1995, cited in Lupton 1997, p. 373)

The notion of self-determination draws from an individualist discourse. Additionally, there is an assumed level of agency in bioethics which characterise actors exercising in their interactions with professionals. However, research has found that people who are involved in decision-making about medical issues are less empowered than those making decisions about other aspects of their day-to-day life (Lupton 1997). In Lupton's empirical study into people's interactions with medical doctors, she found that:

> In their interactions with doctors and other health care workers, lay people may pursue both the ideal-type "consumerist" and the "passive patient" subject position simultaneously or variously, depending on the context…[thus] late modernist notions of reflexivity as applied to issues of consumerism fail to recognise the complexity and changeable nature of the desires, emotions, and needs that characterise the patient-doctor relationship. (Lupton 1997, p. 373)

In Chapter 11 of this book we examine social work and capitalism, including the consumerist model of service provision, however, it is worth noting the ways in which the broader economic structures impact upon the role of the professional. Additionally, the power inherent in medical professionals' roles needs to be understood as related to the degree to which individuals are able to exercise agency.

In social work practice, the value of self-determination or autonomy is often placed at one end of the spectrum with paternalism at the other end. However, the reality of social work roles, particularly those which involve overriding individuals' self-determination such as work with involuntary clients, means that the division between these two seemingly separate ways of working becomes complex. It is therefore argued that the social worker's practice and quality of relationship between themselves and their clients can override this dualism:

Even within a paternalistic environment, by assisting a client to be more self-determining autonomy can be encouraged. This can be achieved through the worker-client relationship, rather than the application of a prescribed set of policies and procedures. (Bowles et al. 2006, p. 141)

Although understanding self-determination as existing in a complex practice environment in which the organisational mandate, client needs and social workers' purposes vary, a more in depth critical lens points to a need to better theorise this concept in social work.

The Problem with Codes

Ethics in social work is institutionalised through professional associations and organisational settings. Alongside the historical professionalisation of social work, the ethical standpoint of the profession has also evolved. Where social work is recognised as a professional activity, a code of conduct or a code of ethics can be found.

In England, for example, the Health and Care Professions Council (HCPC) is the registering body for social workers. One of the requirements for registration is adherence to the Standards of Proficiency, of which the following is noted in relation to adherence to social work ethics:

2. be able to practise within the legal and ethical boundaries of their profession
2.1. understand current legislation applicable to the work of their profession
2.2. understand the need to promote the best interests of service users and carers at all times
2.3. understand the need to protect, safeguard and promote the wellbeing of children, young people and vulnerable adults
2.4. understand the need to address practices which present a risk to or from service users and carers, or others
2.5. be able to manage competing or conflicting interests
2.6. be able to exercise authority as a social worker within the appropriate legal and ethical frameworks
2.7. understand the need to respect and uphold the rights, dignity, values and autonomy of every service user and carer
2.8. recognise that relationships with service users and carers should be based on respect and honesty
2.9. recognise the power dynamics in relationships with service users and carers and be able to manage those dynamics appropriately. (HCPC 2013, p. 7–8)

The language of these standards suggests ethical action is possible if social workers adhere to a prescribed set of behaviours. Though there is mention of the 'dynamics' and 'relationships', there is little significance attached to the meaning, scope and complexity involved in the interpersonal relationship between a social worker and their client(s). The ethical behaviour rests with the social worker, and in such codes of conduct, adjustments are made by the social worker themselves rather than through a process determined through agreement and negotiation with the client(s) (O'Leary et al. 2012, p. 14).

Contemporary social work practice takes place within a model in which the social worker must manage the ethical dilemmas arising out of practice with little specific guidance on how this is achieved (O'Leary et al. 2012, p. 13–14). Codes attempt to provide a meaningful set of statements which are designed to frame practice and address the ethical issues which emerge from the work undertaken. Yet codes are external to the individual: they outsource morality through institutionalised practices. There is considerable critique of codes of ethics. In Bauman's *Postmodern Ethics* (Bauman 1993), the problems of setting the code aside from the individual become clear. Bauman argues that the placement of ethical expectations beyond the individual serves to distance people from their fellow citizens and such distancing allows for the loss of humanity in particular circumstances. Bauman highlights morality as being something which cannot be commoditised or codified and is therefore associated with one's humanness. Here the social work adoption of Rogerian congruence can be a helpful concept to describe the alignment of the person with ethical conduct.

As we see throughout *Sociological Social Work*, there are shifts which have resulted in the dominance of particular ways of knowing and making sense of the world. The positivistic influence of rationality in the field of ethics suggests that the decisions which are associated with, say, doing 'good' deeds can fit into a matrix. Yet human behaviour and circumstances can feel more messy than this. The uniqueness of people and their particular circumstance must be taken into account in decisions about what to do in professional contexts when faced with an ethical dilemma. The question is: how do we respond to ethical dilemmas in a way which promotes social justice and does not serve to oppress? Can or should social workers be doing this? What are the constraints to the processes related to 'doing good'? The answers to these questions are influenced not only by the theories which social workers use to propel them in the world of practice, but by the contexts in which social workers undertake their practice. Ethical social work practice will sometimes involve standing apart from institutional policies or practices or even legal mandates. Just like theories about the world we live in, social policies, legislation and economic and social conditions change. What is interesting about theories surrounding ethics is that ancient influences and traditions continue to exist in contemporary scholarship. Perhaps this is due to ethics' concern with core values and central concerns with questions such as: what is it to live a meaningful life? How do people 'do good'?

In Chapter 4 we discussed Titmuss (1969) in relation to the ways in which welfare is delivered. A strong proponent for universal services, Titmuss argues that this type of state-funded service provision promotes dignity as it avoids stigmatising individuals. Titmuss reminds us that decisions made about welfare affect the fabric of a given society. This is because of the powerful role that leaders have in shaping policies about the degree to which their government will respond to issues such as poverty. How do we – as a society – address social inequality in terms of the unequal distribution of wealth, for example? The provision of universal welfare and subsequent publically funded services is one answer to this question. Other questions include: what is the responsibility of one person towards another who is in need? What is the role of the State? It is important to align such questions with ethics as well as understand that the broader questions about the ways in which social problems such as inequality in relation to material resources, education and health.

These kinds of questions remind us that in understanding the professional responsibilities associated with social workers' day-to-day work, social workers must question and contextualise their work in relation to the ethics of the social and departmental policies and legislation which give them their mandate. This means that although the everyday helps us to better connect the professional self with the self expressed in personal relationships, ethical awareness of broader decisions at national or global levels is required. We now move on to consider global perspectives in relation to social work ethics.

Global Perspectives

The International Federation of Social Workers (IFSW) and the International Association of Schools of Social Work (IASSW) are two social work bodies which represent the increased connection between nations in contemporary life. Global perspectives in relation to ethics help to identify the complex ways in which social work is positioned in organisational settings. The IFSW's Statement of Ethical Principles acknowledges these complexities in the positioning of social work and the potential for this placement to result in dilemmas and ethical conflicts:

> By staying at the level of general principles, the joint IASSW and IFSW statement aims to encourage social workers across the world to reflect on the challenges and dilemmas that face them and make ethically informed decisions about how to act in each particular case. Some of these problem areas include:

- The fact that the loyalty of social workers is often in the middle of conflicting interests.
- The fact that social workers function as both helpers and controllers.
- The conflicts between the duty of social workers to protect the interests of the people with whom they work and societal demands for efficiency and utility.
- The fact that resources in society are limited. (IFSW)

It is crucial that social workers remain aware of the ethical tensions inherent in their work. Social workers in child protection, for example, can find it difficult to work towards the promotion of client autonomy when they are acting in a paternalistic way. The IFSW statement reminds the worker that as 'helpers and controllers' they are in a difficult situation as these roles will invariably clash. As we have argued in this chapter, ethical awareness must occur at both the everyday level as well as inform knowledge about the broader forces which create a space for social work to address social injustice. Imagine, for example, that in child protection social workers had any resource available to them, that is, that they could operate without the budgetary constraints evident in contemporary practice. This access to unlimited resources includes unlimited access to financial help, other professionals' services, housing for clients and so on. Considering whether the practice of the social worker with unlimited resources would differ from a social worker in a contemporary child protection setting helps to flesh out how just how much policy affects the decisions we make in our professional roles which affects the ways in which we interact with our clients.

Some of the literature which we have discussed in *Sociological Social Work* in relation to globalisation and individualisation (Giddens 1991) points to the shift from community to the individual. Additionally, the complexities inherent in the work such as those discussed in relation to child protection, can suggest that social work ethics are difficult to use as anchors to practice. Here Jim Ife's scholarship (2001) is helpful. Ife argues that 'human rights have priority over other claims of right' (p. 8). Human rights have gained prominence as a code which relies upon the connection between people regardless of nationhood, gender, sexual identity, age, disability and so on.

Prominent ethicist Peter Singer (Singer 2009) argues that the decisions we make in our day-to-day life should be connected to the experience of people in other nations or in different circumstances to the actor. Singer argues that the decision to buy a particular brand of product – say a high-end brand product when a less expensive option would fulfil the same function – misses an opportunity to redistribute wealth (Singer 2004). Singer's example draws together two dimensions to ethics which we have discussed in this chapter: the connection between the choices made in everyday life, along with knowledge about broader inequality (for example, poverty and homelessness), are both important in practising and living in an ethically responsible manner.

In this chapter we have argued that everyday ethics rely upon the congruence (Roger 1967) between one's personal life along with their professional world. It also involves an awareness of the broader issues which shape contemporary practice. Social workers rely upon social policy decisions which are ethical. In the next chapter we move on to consider the connections between communities and the importance of social relationships.

Recommended Reading

Banks, S. (2012) *Ethics and Values in Social Work* (fourth edn), Basingstoke: Palgrave Macmillan.

Banks, S. and Nohr, K. (2012) *Practising Social Work Ethics Around the World: Cases and Commentaries*, London: Routledge.

Ife, J. (2001) *Human Rights in Social Work: Towards a Rights-Based Practice*, Cambridge: Cambridge University Press.

Reamer, F. (2006) *Social Work Values and Ethics*, New York: Columbia University Press.

Singer, P. (2004) *One World: the Ethics of Globalisation*, Melbourne: Text Publishing.

Chapter 6
Communities and Social Relationships

Introduction

The distinguished scientist Stephen Hawking opens his book *A Brief History of Time* with the following statement; 'We go about our daily lives understanding almost nothing of the world' (1988, p. ix) from which he makes the case about the value of curiosity, and reminds us of children's rich capacity for the curious. Questions like how is the universe made? How do we know that the earth turns? Why is the sky blue? When asked these questions by a child they can 'astonish us' and bring home how much we can actually take for granted. In short, they can pull us up. Community is a fundamental unit in social work and in some ways it is blue sky. We might not think too deeply about it, if we think about it at all, but it will be familiar to us. Thinking about the taken for granted is the essence of sociological social work.

Consideration of the concept of community, as a social domain and a space for collective relationships, is part of the social work attention to the 'person and/in their environment'. There will be some social workers who have an explicit community development role and so a 'community' sensibility will be in the foreground of their practice (Ife 1997). Social workers may work in community settings, defined perhaps in reference to the identity of the collective group, such as the agency or service target population, young people or older adults. It may be the geographic location that describes 'community', for example community as the borough or suburb, or the region such as the 'Northern community'. Further to this, community resources may be called upon in the social work as supports to a family, group or individual. The social work service may have a community constituency and this may be reflected in the governance arrangements with community management arrangements, or community representatives on a board.

The world we live in is a quickly transforming world, and this will have implications for relational units such as community. Wider trends, technological change and processes of 'globalisation' are altering social relations and the construction of the locality as a space of human interactions, source of identity and 'community'. Increased scholarly attention to these issues seeks to explain them and highlights the impact of anonymous flowing global capital, human mobility, the growth of global media and information systems, and how these contribute to far reaching transformations of the nature of capitalism, governance, agency and social structure (Castells 1989; Bauman 1998). Gidden's analysis, which we discuss more fully in a later chapter, draws attention to 'time/space compression' where social relations can be maintained outside bounded places and across time and space. Castells (1996) maps the changes in social networks, and the rise of a network society as a product of the Digital Information Technological revolution. Against this backdrop questions emerge about how social structures and social life/lives are changing and the consequences for a directional compass for social workers who seek to interpret social life and advance a social justice practice.

In this context the categories in our social work vocabulary need to be unambiguous and perhaps revisited. Sociologists like Beck and Beck-Gernsheim (2002, p. 203) speak of the social world theoretical explanations and categories developed in the modern era as 'zombie categories'. Whilst perhaps the word 'zombie' overstates the case (Martinelli 2003), a zombie image does underscore a need to think about 'community' to better understand the nature of contemporary and unfolding social life, and the form of links and exchanges between micro and macro social systems.

Community is an essential theme running through sociological literature and the subject of work by classical sociologists – Tönnies, Durkheim, Weber, and recent writers like Lois Bryson and Martin Mowbray, Fiona Williams and Zygman Bauman. There is too a lengthy literature on community in social work and community development. Somewhat 'puzzling', and this is noted by writers like Nisbet (1970) and Bryson and Mowbray (1981), community is regularly 'rediscovered' and given tough things to do, like be the social space for solutions to poverty and other social problems. The purpose in the next section of the chapter is not to replicate this material for the reader, but rather to draw on the ideas about community to be found in sociological and social work literature, and the lessons for sociological social work.

Communities and Social Work

Harold Saunders (2005), former United States diplomat, lays out what he calls a new relational paradigm for politics in the twenty-first century. From a background of working in conflict and peace negotiation, Saunders has outlined a coherent set of ideas for political processes where the focus is on ongoing contact and relationships between citizens across diverse communal boundaries. There are traces here of the ideas of Bourdieu which we covered in an earlier chapter. Saunders stresses the value of ongoing relationships as, '…the cumulative experience of interacting' (2005, p. 60), and not one off encounters or contacts. Saunders speaks of this as working in the 'space between':

Each enters the flow of a multilevel process of interaction, not just acting and reacting rationally. As the parties interact, they are developing a common body of experience with each other, an understanding of their interaction, a growing perception of the relationship and certain practices come to be mutually understood (implicit covenants). This process is too complex to be measured, but it can be analysed to the best of human ability provided we name it as worthy of attention in its own right and have a systematic way of organising the analysis. Naming often creates facts that compel attention. Its name is relationship. (2005, p. 61)

Ideas and a practice to support social relationships has been a constant in social work and these ideas reflect the full continuum of ideological perspectives. For example governments of all political hues have placed a community focus on their public policy agendas and done so for varying reasons (Mowbray 2005). The Australian Labor Government, at the end of the Second World War, through the Community Centre Division, instigated a *Community Can Do It* program. One strategy of this program was the formation of Listening Groups. On a Monday between 8.40pm and 9pm the Australian Broadcast Corporation (ABC) broadcast stories of how communities were forming community centres and engaging in other community action. A booklet with key strategies for community development was distributed as an aid for the Listening Groups who sat around the radio. To quote from the booklet:

There's a new spirit abroad – the spirit of community. Maybe it's a revival of an organisation that goes far back into the history of our people. Perhaps we are rediscovering an ideal that we lost, and thereby our democracy suffered and our strength was weakened. The ideals of neighbourliness, mutual aid, co-operation declined when the village community was weakened. (ABC 1945, p. 5)

These efforts under the banner of *Community Can Do It* produced community centres, cooperatives, saw the construction of halls, recreation clubs and swimming pools. Fifty years later and perhaps not dissimilar, is the 2011 UK Cameron Coalition Government's *Big Society* program with a call to neighbours, volunteer groups, and civil society organisations to engage in community work and 'charitable giving':

We are helping people to come together to improve their own lives. **The Big Society is about putting more power in people's hands** – a massive transfer of power from Whitehall to local communities. We want to see people encouraged and enabled to play a more active role in society. (http://www.conservatives.com/Policy/Where_we_stand/Big_Society.aspx)

As well as government measures like those above, in advanced industrial countries there is an increasing phenomena of the commodification of 'community'. In other words people buy a community experience. This is seen in private sector urban housing developments like Master-Planned Estates (MPEs) (McGuirk and Dowling 2007), which are private developments, often on green-field sites or re-developed spaces, where a potential buyer is offered more than the purchase of a property and home, but this *and* a community lifestyle and community values (McGuirk and Dowling 2007). Even though the question can be asked about what this community experience is, it certainly sells land and houses. McGuirk and Dowling (2007, p. 33) note in their work on MPEs in New South Wales, Australia, that it is not uncommon for MPE private consulting firms to offer community development services as a purposeful strategy to build 'community'. Further examples of the marketisation of community can be found in the retail sector, in shared consumption patterns, gated communities, and residential developments i.e. for the growing baby boomer cohort.

We can easily write a long descriptive list of such programs where community has been central. The early settlement movement and the work of Jane Addams, the community movements in Australia and Canada at the end of the nineteenth-century, post-war reconstruction after the Second World War as mentioned above, in the many agendas and actions, including resistant actions of civil society groups, in government funded programs for community building, development and capacity (for instance, the 1960s War on Poverty in the USA, the Australian Assistance Plan in Australia in the 1970s, the *Big Society* initiative of the Cameron government).

Describing Community

One of the messages in the extensive literature on this topic is that community is an ambiguous and slippery idea. 'Communities' are social groupings defined differently: people living in geographic areas, people sharing by virtue of the age cohort they are born into similar life course experiences (i.e. baby boomers or X and Y Generation), school or activity based settings, groups responding to social issues or campaigning, and ethnic and racial groups. Collective actions can be examples of communities opposing or resisting the dominant practices or values of an institution and there have been many examples of this recently across the countries of the European Union in opposition to monetary and austerity policies. Within communities there will be sub groups and also people will identify as members of overlapping communities (Fisk 1993). Nisbet, in 1970, wrote of community:

> Community is a fusion of feeling and thought, of tradition and commitment, of membership and volition. It may be found in, or be given symbolic expression by locality, religion, nation, race, occupation, or crusade. (1970, p. 48)

Expression of communities is changing as people connect across time and space. The community experience in virtual worlds is now extensive and can 'promote a comparable fabric of social connectedness' (Denemark and Niemi 2012, p. 3). Facebook is an example, where friends can communicate to a larger group on as regular a basis as they wish and without leaving home. Virtual communities are located in what Castells writes as 'the culture of real virtuality'. He explains this as follows:

> It is a system in which reality itself (that is, people's material/symbolic existence) is entirely captured, fully immersed in a virtual image setting, in the world of make believe, in which the experiences are not just on the screen through which experience is communicated, but they become the experience. (Castells 1996, p. 373)

Millions of people inhabit virtual communities every day and night. Second Life is a virtual world where humans construct themselves as avatars and in a second life identity engage in recreation, shopping, attend public meetings and live music shows, and form relationships. In many cases the avatar can have an identity and physical characteristics unlike the ones they have in the real world. Capitalism has a presence in Second Life with the exchange of goods and services using a currency called the Linden Dollar. This highlights one of the key characteristics of these 'new' worlds, they retain traces of the 'real world' which are sometimes fragmented, distorted and lagging behind or ahead of developments in the 'real world'. Social media is also an example of other worlds which exist through technological advance. Like Second Life, social media depend upon the creation and maintenance of particular identities and this process is argued as evidence that we are becoming more and more aware of ourselves to the extent that we have turned into our own 'projects' (Giddens 1991).

These types of virtual community experience are growing. As a measure of internet activity in Australia, the Australian Bureau of Statistics reports that 554,771 terabytes of data was downloaded in the three months from October-December 2012, and that this was an increase of 34 per cent from the previous reporting period (ABS 2013). In Britain internet usage is on the rise for e-commerce and service/product purchase, accessing information, leisure and social connections, and for political participation (Dutton and Blank 2012). Dutton and Blank, authors of the *Oxford Internet Survey 2011 Report*, make the comment that 'Use of social networking sites has increased sharply since 2009. This is one of the most dramatic developments in use of the internet in recent years' (2012, p. 33). Usage patterns reflect age, workplaces, computer access, gender, employment status, and income levels, to name some of the influencing variables.

One of the themes Dutton and Blank report on is the digital divide, or in other words the divide between those who use the internet and those who do not. Not having access to a computer, or the means to afford a computer and internet access, are some of the reasons for non-use. The point to be drawn from the above discussion is that there are multiple ways humans will experience community and that new technologies are opening new experiences in virtual spaces, which some will take up and others not.

Descriptions that imply homogeneity of community hide innumerable interests, expression and relations within 'communities' and the whole breadth of subjective accounts of community. Communities are spaces where humans have their identities and talents positively affirmed, and can be spaces of care and love. Research evidence highlights the value of social bonds or social relations for health and wellbeing (CHEX 2009). In a study about a 'Hub' for older people (Verity, Jones and Johnson 2007), a local centre in a district, one of the themes was the self-reported health and social value of the interpersonal relationships formed in the centre. As one older respondent noted, not only does the Hub 'get you out of the house', it offers opportunities to fulfil many social needs, from forming friendships to mutual support in times of crisis. A theme of fellowship enabled through the Hub is evident in the language used by respondents; a language of 'belonging', 'knowing people', 'friends', 'care', 'home' and 'safety'. This is more than being in the presence of others. It implies qualitative interactions of various sorts and in terms mirroring those expressed by Harold Saunders as cited earlier. Some respondents from Verity and Jones's study expressed this connectedness as follows:

> People make and meet their friends here and have a sense of belonging.
> When I was fighting cancer, I couldn't have got through it without the Centre.
> They care for you when you are ill. It is a pleasure working here and my friends are here.
> It is like coming home, my second home. It provides a sense of safety. (Verity, Jones and Johnson 2007)

However, community is not just a space of positive consensual behaviour and experiences; it can be a space of power struggles, envy, conflict and violence, prejudice and hate (Bauman 2000). This aspect of community can be lost in the romanticising of community (Bryson and Mowbray 1981), but inevitably communal relations and conflict go together. People in community spaces will have different views, experiences and hopes. Conflict which does not necessarily imply violence is also an important aspect of voicing opinions and values and challenging dominant ideas and power relations. It is the engine of counter movements. This is seen in the ways that community groups and collectives muster effort to voice and act to challenge oppression and put forward alternatives. The point here is that conflict can never be ironed out of the fabric of social life (Simmel 1971). Hannah Arendt makes this point unmistakably in her work on violence over the course of the twentieth-century: 'No one engaged in thought about history and politics can remain unaware of the enormous role violence has always played in human affairs' (Arendt 1969, p. 111). But how have key sociologists thought about community?

Community Typologies

Gemeinschaft ('Community') and Gesellschaft ('Society')

Ferdinand Tönnies was a nineteenth-century scholar engaged in making sense of the impacts of the industrial revolution in Europe. Tönnies, in his famous book, *Community and Civil Society*, was concerned with social connections, or what he wrote as 'investigating only relationships that are based on positive mutual affirmation' (2001, p. 63). He established two basic constructs of social relations. He named them *Gemeinschaft* ('community') and *Gesellschaft* ('society') with the fundamental difference between them being in the nature of the social relations and the will for the relations. He distinguished between essential will and rational will. On will he writes, 'Since all mental effect, because it is human, is characterised by thinking, I am discerning will inasmuch as it contains thinking and thinking inasmuch as it contains will' (Tönnies 1971, p. 6). Tönnies theorised that *Gemeinschaft* 'community' relations are marked by thick social bonds which implicate mutual obligations, or interdependence and 'shared mores'. These are social relations that are patterned in kinship, and close living and working. As Tönnies writes, these forms of social relations have 'their roots in feeling (in natural inclination and in instinct)' (1971, p. 132):

> Community by *blood*, indicating primal unity of existence, develops more specifically into community of *place*, which is expressed first of all as living in close proximity to one another. This in turn becomes community of *spirit*, working together for the same end and purpose. Community of place is what holds life together on a physical level, just as community of spirit is the binding link on the level of conscious thought. The last of these elements, together with

the former two, is what makes a truly human community in its highest form. In the first type of community we share our common physical humanity, in the second we share land held in common, in the last we usually share sacred places or worship the same deities. All three types of community are intimately connected with each other in respect of both place and time, both in particular phenomena and in the whole of human culture and its history. Wherever human beings are bound together in an organic fashion by their inclination and common consent, Community of one kind or another exists. Either the earlier type contains the nucleus of the later one, or the later one will have developed a relative independence from the earlier. We can regard (1) kinship, (2) neighbourhood, and (3) friendship or comradeship, as perfectly intelligible ways of describing those three original types. (Tönnies 2000, p. 74)

Gesellschaft, or 'associational society', is the term Tönnies used to describe social relations where human inter-relations are a consequence of the exercise of rational will. These forms of social relations will be contractual, mirroring capitalist market contracts and relations in a business and political social contract. Again, with reference to Tönnies:

Society [Gesellschaft]

Big city life convention. This is based on the individual human being with all his ambitions. Its core is *competitive market society in its most basic form.*

National life politics and policy. This is based on man's collective calculations. Its core is the *State.*

Cosmopolitan life public opinion. This is determined by man's consciousness. Its core is the *republic of letters.* (Tönnies 2001, p. 303)

These two notions, *Gemeinschaft* ('community') and *Gesellschaft* ('society'), are thinking constructs and as Tönnies writes: 'I do not know of any condition of culture or society in which elements of *Gemeinschaft* and elements of *Gesellschaft* are not simultaneously present, that is mixed' (1971, p. 10).

From our twenty-first century vantage point, that we have lives where we are engaged in different forms of social relations, and varied intentions for social connections, perhaps seems self-evident. Two residents of the 'neighbourhood' who have different biographies and social experiences will go about their daily routines and interact with people in different ways. Blokland in her book *Urban Bonds* notes that neighbourhood life for some people will be no more than referring to 'the house or shops near where they live' while for others it will be 'community' in the sense of the meaning they place on the interactions they have with others in public spaces (for example shops and parks) and the relations with neighbours. Blokland (2003) further notes a historical trend towards the privatisation of neighbourhood life, in the sense of a move away from a collective and reinforcing identity patterned in neighbourhoods (i.e. based on shared religion, class and work place, or family groupings), or *Gemeinschaft*, and towards a private, individualised choice about where one lives and the nature of relations one needs to have or not have with neighbours. Whether we use public transport, walk around on foot or drive our cars in and out of the areas we live in, all will have a bearing on the relations we form with those we live near.

Chaskin (1997) reports a study by Lee and Campbell (1990) where the social dimension of the neighbourhood was more important in the mental maps for those who spent more time in the neighbourhood (by virtue of age, longevity as residents, or being outside the paid labour market) than those who spent more of their time outside the neighbourhood (because of employment, distance to and time spent at work). The latter group were more inclined to think of the neighbourhood in terms of geographical reference points, like the roads they drive to work on, the park, or shopping centre, rather than maps of social relations. As he says 'One can divide a city in many ways. An individual's construction of his or her place in the large community is complex, changeable, and constantly negotiated' (Chaskin 1997, p. 5).

Bonding and Bridging Social Capital

A further typology of social relationships which has been popular and taken up in many fields of practice is the twentieth-century work of Robert Putnam on social capital. From empirical work on social relationships between people in regions in Italy, Putnam distinguished between types of social capital: bridging and bonding capital. These he defined as the networks and ties between people and the reciprocal relations and trust that exist. Bridging capital is the links between people in communities or social groups not alike, and bonding social capital is the strength of ties within communities of 'people who are like you in some important way' (Putnam 2007, p. 143). Putnam drew on the work of Pierre Bourdieu who defined social capital to be the:

> sum of the resources actual or virtual, that accrue to an individual or group by virtue of possessing a durable network of more of less institutionalised relationships or mutual acquaintance or recognition. (Bourdieu and Wacquant 1992, p. 119)

In Bourdieu's frame social capital is but one form of capital – what he called 'that energy of social physics' (Bourdieu and Wacquant 1992, p. 118) and is located and interacts with economic and cultural capital. The deployment, gains and significance of various forms of capital are related to habitus and field, as was discussed in an earlier chapter. Putnam distinguishes between formal and informal, and weak and strong ties, that will depend on the settings, frequency of interactions and purpose:

> Some forms of social capital are densely interlaced, like a group of steelworkers who work together every day at the factory, go to Catholic Church every Sunday, and go out bowling on Saturday. That is a very dense, interconnected, multiplex form of social capital. There are also very thin, almost invisible forms of social capital, meaning networks and the associated norms of reciprocity, like the nodding acquaintance you have with the person you occasionally see at the supermarket, while waiting in line. (Putnam ud, p. 2)

Putnam also makes the point that social capital is a concept to help one think about social connectedness, and the diversity of these experiences.

Thinking Critically About Community

Thinking critically about community is important in sociological social work. It means we need to think about our own language usage and the mental maps we have of community. This is important so that we do not assume unity and in doing so discount diversity, and that we do not lose sight of complex and interrelated economic, social, racial, and political relations. As Bauman wisely cautions '…let us not be fooled, though, by the apparent commonality of the "safety in community" urges; it glosses over profound differences in socially shaped life conditions' (2000, p. 118). How community is interpreted will depend on one's ideological frame of reference. Bryson and Mowbray in the classic 1981 paper '*Community the Spray-On Solution*' contributed a powerful critique to these debates about 'community'. Community, as they argue, can often be sloppily expressed without explicit discussion as to what is meant by or constitutes community (for example, without spelling out with absolute precision what is being talked about and the agendas), and without exposing underlying assumptions about power relations. They further make the point that in an era of changes in telecommunication and access to cars, the local area for many people has faded as the primary location of community life. Despite this there can be an assumption that community is local area and that it is homogenous. Community is not a proxy for locality.

Fiona Williams (2002) writes of community as 'space' and 'place' to mark out the control aspect of community. Very simply she highlights how 'community' can serve a regulating function of keeping women in their place, i.e. out of politics, in care roles, and financially dependent on men. However 'community' has a contradictory face and she shows how alternatively it can, for women, be a place for the realisation of hopes and aspirations that are beyond the private and personal realm and not delivered by the state (i.e. women's services, supports for domestic and family violence, child care and recreation services).

Iris Marion Young (2000), in her comprehensive discussion of the politics of difference, outlines the ways in which 'community', when connoting unity, can disguise oppression and exploitation of marginalised groups. Attention is needed to cultural heterogeneity. It is more the case now than 40 years ago that many countries have populations that are culturally diverse, a trend predicted to continue (Putnam 2007). There has also been more inter-communal conflict (Craig 1998, p. 8). Such conflict is entangled with political and economic change and race and ethnic relations. Billing, in Adelaide research on media treatment of refugees, draws on the work of Peter Gale who argues that there has been a revival of racism in Australia and that this in part has been fuelled by media debates. Gale calls this revival of racism the 'politics of fear' and traces how it has been driven by media representations and debates about detention centres and refugees. The European Union, in a paper on conflict prevention (2001), in considering this question broadly outlines the many causes of conflict within nations and communities to be '…poverty, inequalities in the distribution of wealth, scarcity and degradation of natural resources, unemployment, lack of education, ethnic and religious tensions' (2001, p. 9).

Plant, in a book entitled *Community,* uses the word 'parasitic' to convey the nature of this relationship between values and perspectives on community (Plant 1974, p. 39):

> The meaning of community is not…given outside any evaluative framework, rather what we take as central to the meaning of community is parasitic upon our general moral and social attitudes. (1974: 37)

This means we consciously think about ideology in relation to community. Eatwell identifies that 'an ideology has an overt and implicit set of empirical and normative views which are goal oriented about 1) human nature; 2) the process of history; 3) the socio-political structure' (1999, p. 14). Thorpe (1985, p. 16), writing a number of years ago delineated between community development approaches using a schema which associates approaches with ideological views (as sets of ideas and beliefs) on the origins of social problems and social change. In her schema, Thorpe distinguishes between community work under a broad structuralist heading that seeks to raise consciousness and where a congruent practice links community development with political action or social movements; pluralist ideologies where advocacy, community planning, participation and action groups constitute the terrain of community work approaches; and consensus political 'isms' where the associated community work approaches are about improving community cohesion and 'community spirit' through self-help and community development. In these three broad ideological approaches there are different views on 'community'; a space and mechanism of unity, social glue and cohesion and reproduction of normative cultural and social values; a space for the articulation of injustices and ideas for social reform and a space of conflicting interests and power struggles for justice, and social change.

Labonte and Laverack (2001a), while supportive of the intentions to build community, argue similarly in stating that promoting community is '…not a panacea to complex social problems arising from unregulated economic globalism' (2001, p. 128). They powerfully remind the reader that a change agenda requires '…an eye on the national and global policy ball' (2001, p. 128). Labonte and Laverack (2001a) make the point that:

> There are groups whose capacity is created primarily by denying the same to others: racists, xenophobes, sexists, totalitarians and, it can be advanced, private (individual or corporate) economic decisions that fail to consider their effects on distributive justice or environmental sustainability. There is a need to make choices over which groups in society should have their capacity increased and claim that the more conscious the choosing the more it is "subject to theoretical, empirical and ethical review". (2001a, p. 127)

Mowbray (2005, p. 263) takes issue with what he calls the 'grandiose' nature of claims that community can be the source of major social change. From his perspective community building fostered by government is more likely to be about '…*strengthening central governmental agendas*' than any actual empowerment developments. Instead, he writes, a concern for empowerment would see governments '…*embark on wholehearted socio-economic reform*' and support practices that are long term, well-funded, and with decision-making power devolved (2005, p. 264).

Throughout these critical perspectives runs a theme of thinking deeply about community, with an eye to ideology, with variations of all types including cultural and religious difference, and to situate any analysis in the broader context of a dynamic social world.

Social relationships are an essential aspect of social worlds. There are multiple ways humans will experience community and new digital technologies are opening new experiences in virtual spaces, which some will take up and others not. In this chapter we canvassed perspectives on community offered by sociological writers and from the critical literature in community development. Community can be blue sky territory in that it can seem so obvious that it is not thought much about. One of the key lessons in a substantial literature is that 'community' can be used in ways that mystify complex and interrelated economic, gender, social, racial and political relations. It can be used to keep people in their place. These contradictions elevate the need to think so that social workers who seek to support communities are clear on their intentions and values. Thinking of community in terms of gender, race and culture, age and other social divisions is indispensable. This also means to contextualise 'community' in the multiple factors which shape the live conditions of people who are in varied social relationships. However difficult 'community' is as a concept, engaging in thinking about diversity in community, especially in respect to diversity in value dimensions is critical. Only by doing this can we be equipped for practices of value base social work.

Recommended Reading

Bauman, Z. (2001) *Community. Seeking Safety in an Insecure World*, Cambridge: Polity Press.

Bryson, L. and Mowbray, M. (1981) "Community: the Spray on Solution" *Australian Journal of Social Issues,* Vol. 16, No. 4.

Nisbet, R. (1970) *The Sociological Tradition*, London: Heinemann.

Tönnies, F. (1955) *Community and Civil Society*, Cambridge: Cambridge University Press.

Putnam, R. (1993) *Making Democracy Work: Civic Traditions in Modern Italy*, Princeton University Press, New Jersey.

Chapter 7
Social Solidarity in the Age of Climate Change

Introduction

Examples of unsettling weather events across the globe are now more frequent and new records are being broken each year. In 2012 North America experienced record heat waves, and in the same year Mediterranean countries had unusually dry winters. In 2010 Russia experienced a heat wave with severe health, social and economic impacts (World Bank 2012, p. 14–15). Recently in Australia, Queensland experienced devastating floods on an unprecedented scale, followed by Cyclone Yasi with wind gusts of 285 km/h (Australian Bureau of Meteorology, http://www.bom.gov.au/cyclone/history/yasi.shtml). Climate change has been especially brutal in Africa, exacerbating the effects of long-term drought and low agricultural yields. When people's livelihoods are reliant upon the ability of the land and climate to provide the conditions for growing food, conditions such as drought are devastating. On a broader scale, drought can be the driver for economic downturn and the movement of people.

This global occurrence of the climate changing brings to the foreground our profoundly shared existence as people who live on the same planet, who will together and differently live through the impacts of extreme weather events. However, we will not experience the effects and adjust to climate change equally. The existing multiple forms of structural injustice – like income and wealth inequality and injustices in life experiences (based in social relations of gender, race, age, economic position, disability, sexual identity, geographical location and other aspects of difference) – will impact on how peoples from different continents, nations, hemispheres, wealth and consumption positions, capacities and knowledge, and health status will unequally experience climate change (Castells 1998; Dominelli 2011; World Bank 2012). Given that social work has a rich history in fighting oppression, the social injustices which are connected to climate change ought to be of concern to social workers. To date there has been little theoretical engagement with the models which can help frame the kinds of social work which are required for this new age.

In this chapter we explore Durkheim's notion of solidarity. As we have argued in *Sociological Social Work*, our profession has adopted increasingly individualist discourses, such as those associated with the therapeutic turn in society (Furedi

1991). In Chapter 3 we examined the social work self and suggested that identity ought to be conceptualised more in line with an appreciation of the powerful role that social interaction, socialisation and biography play, rather than draw from psychoanalytic theories of subjectivity. In this chapter we continue to highlight the role that society plays in individual experience.

The classical sociologist Emile Durkheim has much to offer in this regard. For example, instead of understanding suicide as an individual pathology, Durkheim's famous study analysed the social conditions which led to individuals taking their lives. By comparing suicide rates internationally and how these differed in varying groups in society, Durkheim was able to demonstrate that there was an inverse relationship between taking one's own life and the density of social integration (Durkheim 1897). Alongside social and political influences, Durkheim examined other factors such as marital status and religious membership as relevant to such statistics in suicidality. Such studies are highly useful for social workers, particularly those for whom the reduction of suicide to 'personality deficits' is something they encounter in their practice.

Secondly, we argue that contemporary life offers new opportunities to understand one another across national divisions. The acceptance of cultural difference, which is also referred to as cosmopolitanism, helps to unite people across national boundaries. What Ulrich Beck calls the 'cosmopolitan moment' in our time represents an opportunity for people to come together to make changes which help address climate change. We argue that the notion of solidarity ought to frame social work's response to climate change because it provides a theoretical platform upon which nationhood and the importance of social conditions on individual and community wellbeing can be better understood.

Climate Change

There are a number of greenhouse gases in Earth's atmosphere. Some of these gases are natural and others are the result of human activities, most notably the byproducts of industrialisation processes such as the burning of fossil fuels like coal, oil and gas, and deforestation that has stripped landscapes of trees. Earth's atmosphere is finely tuned and gases in the atmosphere play a vital role in the constitution of the Earth's screen against the ferocity of the sun's rays, and in keeping heat in (NASA 2005). This is a regulating function, rather like the use of blinds in a house that we pull down to keep fierce daytime heat out – but still have the light come in – and at night, to keep heat in the house. Another commonly used analogy is to think about greenhouse gases as the earth's blanket, and one we all share. Yet 'The climate system is highly sensitive to concentrations of greenhouse gases in the atmosphere' (World Bank 2012, p. 22).

A cause of climate change is global warming, with rises in the Earth's average temperature that are related to increased concentrations of carbon dioxide (CO_2) emissions in the atmosphere, as well as other greenhouse gases such as methane fluorinated gases, nitrous oxide, and sulphur hexafluoride (USA Environmental Protection Agency; United Nations 2009; World Bank 2012). In particular, concentrations of CO_2 emissions have been steadily rising in the time from the beginning of European industrialisation, a time that scientists call 'pre-industrial air' to the now of the new millennium. CO_2 levels released into the Earth's atmosphere are at highly damaging levels. Some of these greenhouse gases have what is known as a 'long life' and so they will not dissipate for hundreds or more years. We are now seeing the extreme effects (USA Environmental Protection Agency; United Nations 2009).

In 2013 scientists from the National Oceanic and Atmospheric Administration (NOAA) Mauna Loa Observatory in Hawaii, who systematically monitor greenhouse gases in the atmosphere, announced the fact that:

On May 9, the daily mean concentration of carbon dioxide in the atmosphere of Mauna Loa, Hawaii, surpassed 400 parts per million (ppm) for the first time since measurements began in 1958. (http://researchmatters.noaa.gov/news/Pages/CarbonDioxideatMaunaLoareaches400ppm.aspx)

This peak is an alarming figure and the predications are that such a trend line may well keep rising, but even if it is stabilised, the existing order of the problem will have dire natural, human and animal, economic and social consequences.

The United Nations, in response to this figure of 400 parts per million, issued the following statement:

With 400 ppm CO_2 in the atmosphere, we have crossed an historic threshold and entered a new danger zone. The world must wake up and take note of what this means for human security, human welfare and economic development. In the face of clear and present danger, we need a policy response which truly rises to the challenge. We still have a chance to stave off the worst effects of climate change, but this will require a greatly stepped-up response across all three central pillars of action: action by the international community, by government at all levels, and by business and finance. (United Nations Climate Change Secretariat, 13 May 2013)

Impacts of Climate Change

There is a growing literature charting in detail the aforementioned impacts, with predictions of many health and disease consequences resultant from extremes in temperature and heightened food insecurity; land use effects of drought and floods; extinction of animals and plants, and consequential economic and social impacts (McMichael and Kovats 2000; World Health Organisation (WHO) 2005; Woodruff et al. 2005; Flannery 2005). These impacts are not just predictions, they are occurring now. A reduction in arable land, extended drought, and famine and floods are the preconditions of poverty, people movement, political pressures, anxiety and uncertainty (Beck 2009). These interconnected impacts, and the contributing causal factors, are not so readily teased apart and able to be addressed independently from one another. Climate change fits the definition of a 'wicked social problem', the type of problem Rittel and Weber, writing in 1973, defined as inherently 'tricky' and contested.

There are also predictions of what may occur without concerted global efforts to redress this trend. One is the estimation that the earth faces the risk that global warming could be at a level of 4 per cent by the end of the century (World Bank 2012). The World Bank in a recent report paints a dramatic picture of the possible risks in such a scenario:

> The 4°C scenarios are devastating: the inundation of coastal cities; increasing risks for food production potentially leading to higher malnutrition rates; many dry regions becoming dryer, wet regions wetter; unprecedented heat waves in many regions, especially in the tropics; substantially exacerbated water scarcity in many regions; increased frequency of high-intensity tropical cyclones; and irreversible loss of biodiversity, including coral reef systems. (World Bank 2012, p. ix)

Impacts of climate change are already especially severe for those who are poor and with constrained or limited individual and/or collective means to cushion the impacts of climate change, and/or adapt their homes, means of production, living circumstances and environmental practices as the weather changes (World Bank 2012). For example people who live in low-lying countries or areas with shelter and food production that can be easily destroyed in an extreme weather event; people on low incomes who do not have the resources and cannot afford to pay for the costs of heating and cooling or greener technology; or communities where extended drought pushes them to the brink of disaster and despair.

It is well documented that depression and suicide have been one of the tragic impacts of the prolonged drought in rural and regional Australia. Miller and Burns (2008) provide an estimation of the rate of suicides on farms in South Australia using a measure drawn from an analysis of files in the South Australian Coroner's Court (looking at the suicide of farm residents between 1997–2001) and an estimation of the number of people who live on South Australian farms. They estimate a suicide rate for farm residents in South Australia to be 33.8 per 100,000 for men and 6.7 per 100,000 for women (2008,

p. 327). This is higher than both the rates for rural South Australia and the state as a whole and especially high for men.

The politics of climate change are fierce, as has been evident in the debates across the globe played out in the press, through social media, at various international conventions and conferences, and through the academic literature. Some of the themes in the debates are about the validity and reliability of the science; contested definitions, techniques and interpretations of what are measured reflecting varied political and ethical positions and interests. Other related debates focus on the genesis of climate change and ask the question: is human activity resultant from the activities and practices of industrialisation (pollution, burning of fossil fuels, deforestation), known as anthropogenic influences, or is climate change a naturally occurring phenomenon? (Commonwealth of Australia 2007, p. 5). For example, a view from the latter perspective is that the planet will always experience variations in the climate and the impacts of events, such as solar flares, warm the earth. These perspectives impact the will of vested capitalist interests to implement changes to reduce their carbon footprints, to see that industrial capitalism and its practices is the issue to be changed.

Other debates turn on the vexed subject of what is to be done, where it should be done and by whom, and whose role it is to guide change. Is it an individual householder's responsibility, should the market be taking the lead in changing emissions practices, is it for governments to guide these changes? And which governments; is it a national matter or one that requires international collaboration? Carbon emission trading schemes are in place in some countries, with national debates in countries like Australia about how such schemes should be structured and paid for; efforts are occurring to minimise global carbon footprints and companies are developing green technology (such as solar and wind energy) that does not rely on burning of fossil fuels; individuals and groups are acting 'to think globally and act locally', and there are global agreements. For example the Copenhagen Climate Conference in 2009 settled on an agreement from the participating nations, known as the *Copenhagen Accord,* to hold the rate of temperature increase at 2°C above 'preindustrial temperatures' (2009). The first outcome noted in the Accord is that the parties 'underline that climate change is one of the greatest challenges of our time' (2009, p. 5). The UN states that:

Climate change is a complex problem, which, although environmental in nature, has consequences for all spheres of existence on our planet. It either impacts on – or is impacted by – global issues, including poverty, economic development, population growth, sustainable development and resource management. It is not surprising, then, that solutions come from all disciplines and fields of research and development. (United Nations, http://unfccc.int/essential_background/items/6031.php)

An example of how complicated it is to secure an action agenda is seen in the case example of the tensions about how to adjust to living with less water in the Australian Murray-Darling Basin area. How to live with less water and unpredictable weather patterns in the context of climate change has been the subject of discussion across these communities, and the focus of a process to develop a Basin Plan for water use and allocation, for both human consumption and the environment. The Murray-Darling Basin is an area known as Australia's food bowl, and is home to 2,004,560 people who live across five states and many in regional centres (ABS 2008). For the communities of the Murray-Darling Basin the impacts of living with less water run are located in a historical context of economic restructuring and the removal of tariffs (Murray-Darling Basin Commission 2008), population changes, historical water entitlements and allocations, and climate change with the impact of the long-running drought (Victorian Department of Premier and Cabinet 2009).

High levels of emotion – anger and conflict – between competing interests and difficulties in resolving the issue of water allocation have been constant through the Basin planning process. The authors of a report prepared for the Murray-Darling Basin Commission note that 'Tensions between environmental advocates and farmers overlay tensions between downstream graziers and upstream irrigation farmers. This tension is both social and economic' (Frontier Economics; Tim Cummins and Associates; Watson and Stayner 2008, p. 29). The limitations of national and state governments and the need for new global governance arrangements are also up for debates.

Social Work and Climate Change

Social workers have a crucial role to play in interventions related to climate change, and in some contexts this will be a direct role in climate change mitigation and adaptation, while in other contexts it will be a more indirect role such as working with communities, families and women and men who are experiencing the impacts of climate change. Further still there is a role in advocacy and policy development on matters related to climate change, and a personal role in making changes in carbon footprints and supporting new technologies and community awareness. This is consistent with the tradition in social work of considering the natural environment.

The *Life Model of Social Work* is an example where the organising logic for social work is an ecological model based on awareness of cycles of the natural and social world and the human in relating and adapting to this world. Germain and Gitterman argue that:

> The ecological perspective presents our view that human needs and problems are generated by the transactions between people and their environments. (1980, p. 1)

Further elaborating upon the dynamic which exists between individuals and the social context within which they live, they argue that:

> The ecological perspective provides an adaptive, evolutionary view of human beings in constant interchange with all elements of their environment. Human beings change their physical and social environments and are changed by them through processes of continuous reciprocal adaptation…Physical environments become polluted by man's (sic) release of non-bio gradable matter produced by his technology. (1980, p. 5)

The variations of social impacts arising from climate change and the various governmental arrangements underpin one of the fundamental problems in responding to climate change, namely, how might social solidarity assist? In the following section we examine Durkheim's notion of solidarity and consider this in relation to the needs arising from climate change. As we explored in Chapter 5 in relation to ethics, global perspectives help us connect people together around a shared identity of being human. As we shall see, the concept of solidarity helps us to understand social connectedness in relation to belonging and nationhood. As social workers, solidarity can help to frame global movements and connectedness which informs how social work is undertaken in local structures and contexts.

Durkheim and Solidarity

Emile Durkheim is considered one of the so-called 'founding figures' in sociology, having held the first professorship in the newly formed discipline in the late 1800s. His scholarship on social solidarity is of interest to social work and can be used to inform the ways in which we both understand and respond to our changing environment. In particular, Durkheim's notion of solidarity helps us to understand the ways in which we can come together to achieve social competence and work together towards shared aims.

In his early work, Durkheim focused upon the ways in which modern society is held together by an 'organic' solidarity (Durkheim 1893) that was orientated to the new diversity of roles people had in the industrial age, something sociologists refer to as the division of labour. This differed from the mechanical solidarity that held sway in small scale pre-modern communities which were largely concerned with subsistence agriculture and pastoral ways of life. While understanding this social shift is important to historically situate a variety of social problems such as suicide, it is Durkheim's later work on the universal role of symbols and rituals in terms of an individual's identification with the collective and how unification against social and environmental risks is established that perhaps is most relevant for social workers in responding to climate change. Based on studies of Australian indigenous tribes, Durkheim argued that all societies are characterised by the distinguishing of sacred symbols from mundane objects, with the former being core to ritual celebrations of the collective and the ability of the group to unify during times of crisis. Whereas in indigenous societies this might relate to a time of food shortage with rain dances and use of totems, in contemporary society it may relate to episodes of crisis related to environmental or natural disasters, found during times of warfare or in the aftermath of terrorist acts (West 2008).

Whereas Durkheimian thought on symbols and rituals has traditionally been applied to solidarity within nations, in order to comprehend climate change we need to think how symbols and rituals can imaginatively establish unity and its associated sense of compassion globally. Various social theorists have argued that we need to establish a new kind of social identification such as cosmopolitanism (West 2011; Nash 2008). This requires thinking about the social and political in very different ways, beyond the realm of the nation or culture in which we may feel solidarity or belonging. These themes are salient to the work by Ulrich Beck (2009, p. 49) who has written extensively on risk society. He writes of this time in history as one where there is the possibility to make 'new beginnings' out of catastrophic scenarios. He elaborates on new forms of global risk, like climate change, and spells out how they 'rock the foundations of modern societies' (2009, p. 52) in the way they throw a blanket over the boundaries of nation states, test to the limit the scientific capacities for prediction and certainty given the harmful time life of emissions and especially in respect to social consequences. He writes: 'we are all trapped in a shared global space of threats – without exit' (2009, p. 56). He uses the idea of cosmopolitanism as an invitation into thinking differently and boldly about global social solidarity. We are in the world of climate change together. Such notions extend the national into the global, yet there is evidence that retaining national identity remains important, particularly in the context of natural disaster and environmental crisis:

> Social theory often advances post-national conceptions of cosmopolitanism as the sole solution to global problems. In the context of humanitarianism… an alternative position [highlights the] positive role national cultural sentiment played in Australia's record charitable response to the 2004 South Asian tsunami.

Where the national imaginary in various ways marginalised the other, this cultural distance facilitated charity by international generosity being interpreted as symbolic of the national character and providing cultural resources for fundraising events. The findings…highlight the need for appreciation of the ways technology and risks are mediated by cultural frames. Secondly, they make us attentive to the enduring influence of cultural systems and the limitations of cognitive approaches to comprehending culture. (West 2011)

These ideas of social solidarity have resonance to the social work mission. Global and local are held together. Social and political processes are informed by history, culture, knowledge and wisdom. When joined with scientific facts, and connecting with governmental action, this offers a way to take forward the dialogue, care and compassion, and adjustment that needs to occur. It is also a way to minimise simplistic action and unintended consequences which can happen in situations when one size fits all solutions are used to respond to complex social issues. One of the key drivers in relation to climate change is the way in which we live in our post industrialist society. The negotiations between the market, organisations and corporations, governments and citizens requires careful and yet purposeful action. We cannot think about climate change without an appreciation of social work in a capitalist context and this is addressed more fully in Chapter 10.

Recommended Reading

Beck, U. (2009) *World at Risk*, London: Polity.
Flannery, T. (2005) *The Weather Makers*, London: Penguin.
International Bank for Reconstruction and Development (2012) *Turn Down the Heat: Why a 4°C Warmer World Must be Avoided*, A Report for the World Bank by the Potsdam Institute for Climate Impact Research and Climate Analytics, Washington: The World Bank.

Part 3
Social Work Identity, Self and Agency

Chapter 8
Time: Not What it Used to Be?

What does a chapter about *time* have to offer contemporary social work practice and contribute to the objectives of this book, which are about sociological social work? And why do we think it is worth you taking the time to read and think about time? It would not be surprising to hear you say that any practitioner would know an effective, ethical and thoughtful social worker needs the resources of time. There is never enough time to do all that is required to competently perform the social work role, and this is so much more the case within a neo-liberal social services context and compliance regime and in a world 'speeding up' (Lemert 2007). As was discussed in an earlier chapter, organisations increasingly expect time to be given to completing administrative functions, whether this be recording statistics, acquitting grants, compiling reports and answering emails. This is time away from social work practice and the type of sociological social work analysis we consider to be critical. It also has a negative impact on the health and wellbeing of social workers. For example Arches (1991) conducted a study of burnout in 275 social workers in Massachusetts and found that variables significantly related to burnout and stress for social workers were the 'perception of autonomy' and the rigidity of the organisation. The role of the funding requirements was also a factor that was associated with social work fulfilment. These all have time use impacts.

But perhaps even more fundamentally, before we can answer the question 'what does *time* have to offer contemporary social work practice?', we must ask another question: 'what is meant by time?' Is time a natural earthly dimension, the chronological movement 'from the past through the present to the future' ticked over by the measuring instruments of a clock, mobile phone or Tablet, whichever our preferred time piece. The sun sets and rises and the Earth moves on the path of its orbit around the Sun. Time is a unit of science that measures this. Is time a philosophical and social construct that is given meaning through normative cultural and social practices and ideas within a certain society, which are again made manifest through the possibilities offered by the technological tools of the age; the sundial, hourglass, medieval clock piece, Greenwich Mean Time, and virtual time. Sociologist Barbara Adam has written extensively on time and makes the case in her theorising for a multi-view of time; natural time and time as social time (Adam 1990). She writes:

Time is our destiny because we live our lives unto death and in the knowledge of this inevitability...Time is not only a necessary aspect of change but also of stability, since the latter is nothing but an awareness that something has remained stable while its surrounding environment, and even the components within, have changed. In addition to change and stability, time is central to order since, as Moore (1963, p. 8) observed, without a temporal order there is no order at all. (1990, p. 9)

Adam persuasively argues the value of more consciously thinking about time rather than 'taking it for granted'. She writes: 'Even social scientists charged with the explanation of social life tend to take time for granted, leaving it unaddressed as an implicated rather than an explicated feature of theories and empirical studies' (2004, p. 3). The same can be said for the attention to time in social work. Time is underplayed in social work literature, even though senses of time are implicit in the rhythms and relations of practice. There are some social work models, like Germain and Gitterman's *Life Model of Social Work* (1980) where time as the biological course of a life in reference to social contexts is the organising structure. This particular model is based on an ecological perspective or 'the reciprocal relations between organism and environments' (Germain and Gitterman 1980, p. 28).

In this chapter we focus on time and social work in a world where changes in technology are impacting experiences of time (Castells 1996; Melucci 1998). Castells writes time is now experienced in new ways 'linked to the development of communication technologies' (1996, p. 429). Following Adam's cue we write about time because it is, we suggest, a way into thinking sociologically, and especially to think about what we may not think about or take for granted in a changing social world. Opening a window on time is to open a window on the contours of social lives, the diversity of social experiences across life courses, and concurrent social worlds. Given the core of the social work purpose the insights that may be gained through thinking about time have implications for social work responsiveness. One example is social work's responsiveness to human social development over the course of one's life. Societal changes mean that time pegged life course markers are less suitable predictors and markers of human development. In addition to the work of Adam, in this chapter ideas about time are examined including those in Castells' writings, with reference to the work of Anthony Giddens. We canvass how greater consciousness about time can be a tool for twenty-first century social work imagination and practice, which is the essence of sociological social work.

Social Work and Time

Once we become aware of it, we are left in no doubt that the largest part of Western industrial everyday life is time (Adam 1990, p. 104).

We all have experiences of what Adam writes of as the use of time to regulate everyday life, and she writes comprehensively about this. To apply her logic to social work, the day of the social worker starts with awakening at a certain time and travelling to work, appointments are slotted into the workday up to the time that is set aside to be the lunch break, for a certain duration until the time comes to end the work day and join the traffic heading home. Time is measured by units (days, weeks, months) with a regular ordering of events and rituals marking the annual passage of time, staff meetings, holidays, annual planning conferences to name but some. Durkheim identified time as a 'social fact' in any society and social markers of time lend credence to time seen in this way. Social work is saturated through by time references. In social work practice we draw on ideas of time, including our own responses to time, whether we are aware of this or not. The social worker and the persons, families and community groups engaging with the social worker all bring to their encounters a sense of and connection to time. Melucci call this the internalised rhythm of time. Psychologists Philip Zimbardo and John Boyd have identified six time perspectives that humans might hold: past-negative, past-positive, present-fatalistic, present-hedonistic, future, and transcendental future (2008, p. 52). These are shaped by 'attitudes, beliefs and values related to time' (2008, p. 52). Throughout social work are interactions with people whose time perspectives and patterns will vary. People have been born and raised in social times where temporality was different and this will shape the above mentioned attitudes, beliefs and values.

Time as a measurable resource structures the activities of the social work day, week, and year, as well as the cycles of practice; the beginnings, middle and endings of interventions. Time ideas too profoundly influence the context of practice; what happens within organisations and wider societal institutions. At an organisational level a visible indicator of this is the enterprise bargain agreement about hours of work, and within this the time allocation and structure of social work with those who use services. The day of the social worker who is a counsellor or caseworker will most often be broken into sessions that last a certain time. At the end of the time the session will end, until the next session (Germain and Gitterman 1980).

Taylor in his *Theory of Scientific Management* in the 1930s used time to measure, structure and control the labour activities within the Ford Motor company, a practice that has been hugely influential in recent public sector reform. In Taylor's time-and-motion mentality, efficient time use is productivity, and productivity is profit. In contemporary social work grant funds are provided for specified time periods and come with expectations of outputs/outcomes to be delivered within this time. Accountability is measured this way. There is increasingly attention given to compliance where organisations can spend quite considerable amounts of time in complying with the red tape of funding regulations.

Furthermore, various social work models require certain time perspectives to be central. In crisis intervention the social worker operates from a dominant temporal order of the present, or the 'here and now' of the crisis. The social worker engages in the moment to respond to acute pain and distress. Germain and Gitterman write:

> Time is a significant aspect of service to be considered in contracting. Crisis theory underscores the importance of rapid response to need and suggests the usefulness of brief, focused and immediate service with frequent sessions until the crisis is past. (1980, p. 59)

An example may be the social worker in a hospital emergency department who sees the incoming patient and their family or support system. The social worker using this approach may only see the client for a certain period of time and relate to the physical and socio-emotional needs of the moment. But as well as the present, embedded in practice approaches, will be a view of the future, to the time when the crisis has passed, and what needs to be in place to support the progress out of the crisis. The past is also not absent. In the assessment, case histories or notes will be chronological accounts of what has occurred in historical time. Whilst the present is dominant, simultaneously the social worker will operate with various views of time in mind and within the organisational structure of clock time.

In contrast community social work, or community development, has a different time emphasis. Community development supports collective concerns that prefigure collective action for purposeful social justice developments. Whilst there is a similar social work focus on the presenting issues of the 'here-and-now', and these will be the reasons why people come together, from the outset the time gaze is three focal. One view of time is to the years ahead, to the worlds of a next generation and the generations beyond. To bring about positive change in housing, creation of employment options, local support services, spaces for children to play, a cleaner and safer local environment, healthy food supplies, a new set of social arrangements, time is needed. Together with this future imaginative gaze, community development processes need the passage of time to develop meaningful connections between people who care about similar issues but are yet to meet. It takes time for human encounters to move to a collective project and again, not just time as weeks or months. Trust to work together is not something that happens overnight.

The third time lens in community development is a considered understanding of the past. This is needed to understand how the present has been arrived at in order to challenge and change systems and structures. This is a historical sensibility that C. Wright Mills refers to, as did Gramsci and Marx before him. The problems that manifest in poverty are historically located, and change will be ineffectual without a consideration of what has been reproduced in social relations over time to bring about and sustain poverty. The matter of childhood obesity rates increasing can be seen differently if the time gaze is to the past and to the changing patterns of human food supplies, consumption and affluence.

We have talked in this book about the importance of the social worker engaging in reflective practice, as a process of introspection and critical analysis and an aid to future practice. Reflective processes require a space within which the social worker can recall and revisit past practice encounters, and think and reflect upon them, and analyse what can be changed in the future. This means having a time set aside, a space in a busy day or week that is uninterrupted and conducive to reflective activities in order to take reflections beyond the superficial or surface recall. One of the issues we addressed in an earlier chapter is that often the time needed for this sort of practice is squeezed; there is not enough time in agencies that employ social work and our heads can be crowded.

A final example of the relevance of thinking anew about time is related to the various theories of human development that would be familiar to social workers. Erik Erikson's stages of psychosocial human social development model is an example where life-course markers are built around normative social and cultural expectations of what a human would achieve and be challenged by and resolve, at certain times of a life. This is an epigenetic map of developmental stages over time that unfolds in a sequence. This work was first published in 1950 and still has currency in social work today.

One of the points Erikson makes is that 'the human life cycle and man's (sic) institutions have evolved together' (1950, p. 250). Today life-course markers and societal institutions are out of step with each other, and most certainly Erikson's time frames of what humans will do when, speaks to another time. Consider one example. In Erikson's schema young adulthood is a life stage where the psycho-social challenge is to form an intimate relationship and to make a commitment to another person. In his language this is expressed as marriage and moving away from the place in which they were brought up. Societal institutions are now different, as is human experience. The UK Office for National Statistics reported that in 2011 almost 3 million young adults aged between 20 and 34 were living with parents, and this figure is a substantial increase from 1997 figures. This upward trend is shown in the figure below. A similar trend is evident in Australia and the reasons for this include housing shortages and financial pressures, making it less affordable and even possible to live elsewhere.

Thinking About Social Time

As mentioned earlier Adam has written much on time. In her substantial work she argues for holding an integrative perspective on time that simultaneously

National Statistics Labour

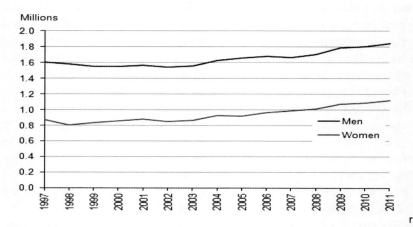

Figure 8.1   Young adults living with parents in the UK, 2011

Source: Labour Force Survey, Office for National Statistics licensed under the Open Government License v. 1.0.

recognises time in all its complexity, and that this unified view – rather akin to the kaleidoscope metaphor we introduced in earlier chapters – can assist 'seeing the invisible' (1990, p.169). This is an inter-disciplinary undertaking drawing in and holding insights from the physical and social sciences. She eloquently writes of the complexity of time as thus:

> Time is found to represent a multitude of phenomena. These include physical entropic processes; life processes of growth, decay and information processing; mechanical, biological, and human social interactions; natural and societal rhythms; novelty and becoming; selves with identities, memories, social histories; and capacities to communicate and synthesise. They encompass calendars, mechanical and atomic clocks; the motion of particles and light; and speed, velocity and acceleration. (1990, p. 43)

and

> We *are* time and this fact unites us with all other rhythmically organised beings. Together with plants and animals *we are aware* of time and experience it. As human beings *we have a relationship to time* and we reckon time. As members of Western industrial societies *we create time* as a resource, as a tool, and as an abstract exchange value. (Adam 1990, p. 161)

A mark of the times we are living in is the 'speed' of living or a sense of immediacy and pace in contemporary life. Expectations are for things to happen now, or at least soon after the now, and we are presented with information and communication at a tremendous pace, whether it is emails in our inboxes, texts on our phones, or an array of requests, images, facts, instantaneous news, and messages through various forms of the media, including social media. Technology has made this possible and it is changing our social world and the nature of social relations. The impacts of time speeding are ubiquitous and it is this that sociologist Lemert defines as a distinguishing feature of our times, and the engine of social change as transformative.

Another take on time is in recent work by the sociologist Manuel Castells in his thesis on the rise of a network society in the context of an information revolution. He employs the idea of 'timeless time' and considers this to be a dominant time perspective that is structuring social life in all forms. This view of time is a break from viewing time as only a linear sequencing of past, present and future. Time is at the same time random and instant. Examples Castells uses are 'split second financial transactions' that bounce across the world and 'the blurring of the lifecycle', a theme which we canvassed earlier (1996, p. 464). Castells writes:

> I propose the idea of timeless time, as I label the dominant temporality of our society, occurs when the characteristics of a given society, namely, the informational paradigm and the network society, induce systemic perturbation in the sequential order of phenomena in that context. This perturbation may take the form of compressing the occurrence of phenomena, aimed at instantaneity, or else by introducing random discontinuity in the sequence. Elimination of sequencing creates undifferentiated time, which is tantamount of eternity. (1996, p. 464)

Related to what Castells proposed are Giddens' notions of distanciation and disembedding which are ways to describe time and space compression. Distanciation is the 'conditions under which time and space are organised so as to connect presence and absence' (Giddens 1990, p. 14). Disembedding refers to the changing nature of social relations which can be maintained across time and space. This is evident in forms of global information such as when an event on the other side of the world can stop the activities of people living in different time/space zones. The impact of the death of the Princess of Wales and the immediacy of the reaction for people living in Australia, who heard about this before people in the UK woke, is a case in point. We return to these themes of time and space compression in the next chapter.

But there are counter reactions to speed and how this is changing social life and social relations. One example is a, now quite extensive, global movement urging humans to 'go slow'. This is to be slower in taking time to think, communicating, shopping or growing, preparing and eating food ('slow food' as distinct from 'fast food'), in parenting and care roles, and in interactions with friends and family. Carl Honore, author of *In Praise of Slowness: How a*

worldwide movement is challenging the cult of speed, made these comments on a recent
Australian radio program:

> **Carl Honore:** Well I think our addiction with speed is carrying us into absolutely
> absurd lengths nowadays. Near my house in London is a gym that offers an
> evening course now in Speed Yoga. It's for time-starved professionals who want
> to salute-the-sun bend their bodies into the lotus position, but they want to do it
> in 20 minutes instead of a whole hour. And I thought that Speed Yoga was the
> most ludicrous manifestation of this road-runner culture until a friend of mine in
> the United States got invited to a Drive-Thru Funeral. Church places coffin at the
> entrance, people pull up in their cars, wind down the window, throw flowers, say
> goodbye, and off they go...it's like getting a Big Mac at a drive through McDonalds.
> A couple of months ago I did talk at a church in Vienna, Austria, and afterwards
> the Monsignor, the head of the church came up to me slightly sheepishly, and he
> said, "You know, when you were talking I suddenly realised how easy it is for all of
> us to get caught up in this speed approach", and he said to me, "You know, when
> you were talking I suddenly realised that I'd been praying too fast". We've got to
> the stage where even Monsignors high up in the church are praying in fast-forward
> then we've really lost our bearing. (ABC Radio National, Future Tense, 2010)

Honore and colleagues in the slow movement propose strategies like consciously
being mindful of the pace of life and the use of time, and resisting the urge for
speed. As social workers we know this is easier said than done. This GoSlow
movement does illustrate, however, the counter narratives and movements at
work alongside the normative expectations and preoccupations. To think about
going slow is a useful way to think about how time is ordering and pacing social
work, and the opportunity costs in going ever faster.

As we have explored in this chapter, time is a rich area of scholarship. It
has preoccupied scientists, philosophers, sociologists and encompasses many
things all at once. Time is clock time, date referenced, which advances second
by second and minute by minute marking the passage of day to night and night
to day, season to season as the earth spins and rotates on its orbit around the
sun. Time references the linear and measurable progress that has been called
BC to AD, millennium to millennium.

Time is also social time. It orders social worlds and how this happens reflects
the technology of these social worlds. In our time of digital technological capacity,
and the possible inventions just on our doorstep, the speed and randomness of
time, as Castells suggests, is something that will change the world. There are
however counters to these dominant trends such as the GoSlow movement.
There are also people who are not connected to the digital information world
and their experiences of time might well be different to those connected to
social media and engaging in other forms of online communities.

All of this has implications for social work. Thinking about time is a way to think about the diversity of human experience and the interactions with social structures and the micro social worlds in which people live.

Recommended Reading

Adam, B. (1990) *Time and Social Theory*, Cambridge: Polity Press.

Castells, M. (1996) 'The Rise of the Network Society', *The Information Age: Economy, Society and Culture, Vol. 1*, Oxford: Blackwell.

Giddens, A. (1987) 'Time and Social Organisation', *Social Theory and Modern Sociology*, Cambridge: Polity Press.

Chapter 9
Social Work in Late Modern Space and Time

Building on from the material covered in the previous chapter, we now examine contemporary social work as situated in late modern space and time. The application of sociological theories which relate to the current historical epoch help to frame social work as a profession. This knowledge also feeds into a broader consideration of individual social work identities or selves. The application of sociological theory about space and time is so crucial to practice that is responsive to, and analytical of, the challenges which present themselves now and into the future. Time and space are argued as under-theorised and underappreciated mediators of the social work task as we shall see through the consideration of agency, temporality and spatiality.

Late Modernity, Contemporary Life and the Now

Much has been written about contemporary life and the impact of new social forms upon the individual. We shall explore some of the key ideas from such scholarship and make some suggestions as to how these ideas relate to social work. It is important to explore some of the key theoretical themes which arise in an examination of the literature which relates to contemporary life.

Firstly, in order to understand how time and space can be invigorated and theorised in social work, one must understand how periodisation helps to create particular threads which, when woven, form history. The naming of particular movements and eras helps to frame the idiosyncrasies associated with a range of periods in time. When we think about the 1960s, for example, we are likely to associate it with the women's rights movement, particular styles of music, fashion, art and architecture. Similarly, the 1970s evokes specific movements in art, fashion, design and politics. Sometimes reflecting on these eras evokes a recognition of one's own history: a child of the 1980s will recall different examples from the 1980s which characterise the era than say a child of the 1970s who is thinking about the 1980s.

One of the key theorists of late modernity is Anthony Giddens (1984; 1990; 1991; 1992), whose work from the mid-1980s into the 1990s signals a major theoretical tradition which influenced sociological thinking about our contemporary world. Giddens argues that macro-economic changes brought about through globalisation have impacted individual relationships as well as the ways in which we think about our sense of self. Giddens argues that our new individualised world constructs selfhood as an 'ongoing project' (Giddens 1992, p. 30) in which all forms of time come together to realise this project. He says:

> The self today is for everyone a reflexive project – a more or less continuous interrogation of past, present and future. (Giddens 1992, p. 30)

For Giddens, reflexivity is central to late modern life. We explored theories of reflexivity in Chapter 3 of this book through an examination of the social work self. What is important to note in the context of our exploration of social work in late modern time and space, is the ways in which the self is conceptualised through reflexive activities which are argued to provide a meeting point for the past and future as well as the present.

Whilst Giddens' argument notes the connection between time and reflexivity, underpinning this idea is a self which is constructed through cognitive processes and deliberate self-fashioning. As Smith notes: 'for individuals, the lifespan and personal biographical work…becomes a self-referential project, dislocated from traditional grounding in locality, kinship, community and ritual passage' (Smith 2002, p. 44). This process is argued to disembed the self away from traditional ties (Giddens 1991). However it ought to be noted that Giddens' theory of the project of the self in late modernity (Giddens 1991) is contested (Alexander 1996; Skeggs 2004; Jackson 2010; Adams 2003) and points to a particular stance about identity, reflexivity and late modern time and space.

On the other hand, the interactionist notion of self – as discussed in Chapter 3 of this book – is a theoretical tradition which argues that the self is produced through social interaction (Mead 1913). For Mead, the self is grounded through interaction rather than disembedded. Alongside post-structuralist constructions of self, Giddens' thesis of late modernity and its subsequent theory of self is often seen as preferable to Mead's scholarship around selfhood (Jackson 2010): this is to the detriment of the social sciences. As we have argued, Mead's concept of self ought to be of greater interest to social work and has been sidelined by the therapeutic turn in recent decades (Dunk-West 2013). George Herbert Mead's theory of self and scholarship which theorises time and the self is relevant here as we shall see.

To get back to the key social developments in recent times, one of the pervasive ideas is that we live in a risky place, full of uncertainties. Risk is arguably everywhere in late modernity (Beck 1992) and has been so embedded into the fabric of our everyday lives that it often goes unchallenged. The concept of risk informs 'safeguarding' work with children, adults and people considered vulnerable, for example. Research highlights the ways in which risk has become individualised, which reinforces discrimination and violence as the responsibility of the individual rather than society itself (Leaker and Dunk-West 2011). Other research suggests that risk is severely limiting the ways in which social work services are provided, or if they are provided at all, due to public liability insurance and perceived levels of risk (Verity 2006). Risk is an example of a concept which is linked to contemporary life and is largely accepted as a valid and necessary process whereby our social situations can be mediated, assessed and used to protect individuals, groups and communities. There are many other examples of phenomena which occur in day-to-day life which are idiosyncratic to our current age.

Giddens' work identifies some of the key shifts which impact upon the ways in which we interact in everyday life. For example, the move away from tradition, for Giddens, signals a change in the way individuals relate to one another. The process of de-traditionalisation has had profound effects for men and women as their roles have become less socially prescribed and more negotiated (Giddens 1990; 1992). Individualisation relates to the ways in which the individual must make an array of choices – historically not available to them – in their day-to-day lives (Beck 1992). For some theorists, such shifts are to the detriment of human relationships. Bauman, for example, describes the liquidity inherent in contemporary times (Bauman 1998; 2000) and this coming together of complex social conditions has had a negative impact upon the ways in which we experience intimacy. Bauman argues that:

> In our world of rampant "individualization" relationships are mixed blessings. They vacillate between a sweet dream and a nightmare, and there is no telling when one turns into the other…In a liquid modern setting of life, relationships are perhaps the most common, acute, deeply felt and troublesome incarnations of ambivalence. (Bauman 2003, p. viii)

Not only are the ways that we relate to one another theorised to have dramatically changed or even deteriorated, the mechanisms we use to engage with one another and the world around us have and continue to change at a fast pace. Indeed, quick technological expanse is perhaps the most easily recognised signifier of the shifting social landscape within which contemporary life is immersed.

The rapidity of developments in technology which are then realised through consumer products means that tangible change occurs within a period of years as opposed to taking decades or generations. Children being raised today are amongst the first generation to grow up with the internet and subsequent devices and platforms which connect people in new ways. The speed at which an email arrives seems to have sped up time itself (Lash 2001). Like other aspects of contemporary life, a critical analysis is helpful in understanding how the profession and the professional make sense of these developments. Therefore in social work it is vital for practitioners to engage in a sophisticated level of analysis: 'a science of social work would encourage critical appraisal of all technologies: Do they do more good than harm? Have they assumed a life of their own in which we no longer question their effects?' (Gambrill 2012, p. 485). Gambrill's latter point suggests the adoption of a sociological imagination (Mills 1959) in which the individual social worker thinks more broadly about the social meanings, consequences and complexities related to technological advance. Similarly, it ought to be a central role of social work to better understand how technologies shift space and time.

The child protection social worker uses technology in their everyday practice, for example, to input assessment data into a centralised computer database and perhaps even to categorise risk. Yet at the same time, they are simultaneously drawing from rationalist frameworks in which risk is assessed. For example, a parent's harmful behaviour in the *past* influences decisions made *today* about the welfare of the child in the *future*. A recent analysis of child protection and time highlights the temporality inherent in assessments which shape social workers' actions and reactions. Fahlgren offers a discourse analysis of time and child welfare work and notes that if 'social work seems to be carried out according to a time order that implicitly assumes improvement with/over time without achieving noticeable normalisation, then forceful intervention is considered justified. The longer the abnormality has persisted, the more forceful the intervention allowed' (Fahlgren 2009, p. 211). Although these practices apply to situations involving risk including risk of life, a critical engagement helps us understand the ways in which social work embeds notions of temporality in its work. In analysing the underlying assumptions which characterise particular ways of conceptualising temporality, increased awareness of difference becomes possible. Fahlgren argues that a linear model of time is unhelpful for clients and results in child protection approaches which are 'cruel' and simplistic (Fahlgren 2009).

Such work highlights the need for social work students to learn the skills to unravel the inbuilt assumptions of the ways in which social work is arranged in its organisational context. For example, social work becomes more accountable to the people with whom it works by recognising the culturally-specific and socially-sanctioned ways in which linear time is embedded in everyday interactions.

The role that space has played has perhaps been better accounted for in social work scholarship. The location of the individual in their social context is a recurring theme in social work which dates back to its beginnings (see, for example, Siporin 1972; Shulman 2009) and sets it aside from other professions such as in health or psychology. To continue with the example of social work practice in a child protection context, parents might be assessed in their social and spatial contexts which can have an impact upon the ways in which they are responded to by social workers. The removal of a parent to a residential facility where they can engage in educative and therapeutic interventions is an example of this. Notably, however, in this example, the social workers are controlling the spatial location of their clients so that surveillance and assessment can be amplified in a particular setting.

Additionally, the context within which the behaviours are analysed may relegate space as a reference point. Social workers must therefore consider their practice in relation to not only the client's relationship with space and time, but the orientation of the organisation, the work itself and the social work role depends upon the ways in which time and space are constructed:

> ...the literature of social work and welfare practice still lacks context as to how practice actually goes on within time and space. It is as if patients can be treated, offenders rendered safer on probations, adults helped and children protected without professionals ever having to leave their desks. The key point is that nothing is seen to be moving, in the literal sense that such practices require the mobility of human bodies, information and objects such as cars. (Ferguson 2008, p. 562)

Importantly, time and space is constantly in flux: their meanings change across different contexts in the so-called 'mobile' world.

Space and New Mobilities

The ways in which individuals live in the world around them has arguably never been of more interest to researchers and scholars than in the present era. There is now a considerable scholarship which is relevant to a sociological social work of spatiality and the self. For the purposes of this chapter we have limited this discussion to issues which are immediately relevant in the social sciences, yet it ought to be noted that there is a great deal of further research and scholarship that is yet to emerge in social work which examines literature from other areas such as the pure sciences and geography.

The study of mobilities in an increasingly complex world (Urry 2005; Urry 2007) notes that travel of varying forms requires theoretical and empirical attention (Büscher and Urry 2009):

> All social life, of work, family, education and politics, presumes relationships of intermittent presence and modes of absence depending on part upon

multiple technologies of travel and communications that move objects, people, ideas, images across varying distances. Presence is thus intermittent, achieved, performed and always interdependent with other processes of connection and communication. (Büscher and Urry 2009, p. 101)

Since we have stressed the importance of connections, interactions and relationality to everyday life and wellbeing throughout this book, the new movements in relation to space and time are relevant to both the ways people interact and move through the world around them and also to the changes in the ways people relate to one another. As we saw in Chapter 7, the emphasis of the 'global' in articulating an identity and a common meeting point for societies across the world should not eclipse the continuing role of national identities in drawing people together in the face of, for example, environmental disaster and crisis (West and Smith 2008).

In popular culture, the national context has been woven into explorations of identity. Perhaps the best example of this was the popular HBO television series, *Sex and the City*. Broadcasting commenced in the late 1990s and the subject of the series was the intimate and sexual interactions of four women. Set in New York city, the central character's ruminations about her relationships – articulated as questions posed in her fictional newspaper column – epitomise the reflexivity associated with the 'self as project' (Giddens 1991). Importantly, the relationship between the characters and New York city was crucial to their identities. The title says it all: 'Sex *and* the City', not 'Sex *in* the City'. Richard Florida's international bestseller *Who's Your City* highlights this tendency towards increased mobility, the project of selfhood (Giddens 1991) and increased awareness of geographic spatiality and national symbiosis with the self. He says:

> Place remains the central axis of our time – more important to the world economy and our individual lives than ever before. As the most mobile people in human history, we are fortunate to have an incredibly diverse menu of places – in our own country and around the world – from which to choose. That's important because each of us has different needs and preferences. Luckily, places differ as much as we do. Some have thriving job markets, others excel at the basics, like education and safety. Some are better for singles, others for families. Some are more about work, some play. Some lean conservative, others liberal. They all cater to different types, and each has its own personality, its own soul. (Florida 2008, p. 7)

In this final section of the chapter we consider the degree to which individuals are able to exercise choice about space and time by exploring the agency versus structure debate. We consider the limitations brought about by gender in better understanding the concept of 'choice' in our contemporary world.

Gender, Agency and Structure

The ambiguity about the structure and nature of day-to-day life has been associated with the period of time which we find ourselves in currently (du Gay 1993, p. 583). As we have seen, there are new patterns of movement and these 'scapes and flows' point to a new 'mobility' (Urry 2000, p. 13). For some, the period of feminism which saw women engage in how to 'liberate themselves from the home' (Giddens 1991, p. 216) was instrumental in bringing about social shifts in the social prescription of gender roles.

In considering the new mobilities which are associated with late modern space and time, it is important to consider how factors such as race or culture, class, gender, sexual identity, disability and other aspects of difference are realised. Factors such as class and gender cannot be excluded from theories in which late modern conditions are understood (Adkins 2003; Skeggs 1997). Such an analysis helps to frame social work in the orientation towards working with difference but questions the veracity that de-traditionalisation occurs at all, or even that it occurs for a few but not all.

For example, Brooks argues that there is a lack of evidence that gender has been 'de-traditionalised' (Brooks 2008, p. 539). Connell understands hegemonic masculinity through the nation (Connell 1987), and is analysed in the context of global shifts (Beasley 2008; Connell and Messerschmidt 2005). The role of the global, the national and gender need to come together for a full analysis. For example, in understanding nation and sport-based violence, it is essential to examine it alongside theories of masculinity (see, for example, Newburn and Stanko 1994). In short, aspects of difference such as gender, but also class, race and culture, disability and sexual identity all require careful contextualisation.

An example of the importance of taking late modern social conditions into consideration can be seen through the proliferation of risk narratives (Beck 1992) in contemporary culture. This has meant that social events, services and everyday transactions are seen through the lens of risk. This has meant the application of judgement about what is 'risky'. Without a critical lens and appreciation that this is, in fact, occurring, risk can become individualised which diminishes the political importance of the application of risk to certain groups in society. The recent 'risk turn' (Walklate and Mythen 2010, p. 45), for example, has been found to individualise risk to the detriment of a broader understanding of socio-cultural, gendered risk as it relates to sexual behaviour (Leaker and Dunk-West 2011).

Another aspect to time and space as situated in late modernity is to consider the relationship between the individual and society. Thinking about agency and structure involves asking questions such as the following: which is 'stronger', the individual or society? Can an individual go against socially prescribed roles? What are the impacts of society on individual choice?

Yet overlapping, opposing and contradictory sociocultural scripts continue to dominate the public sphere (Jackson 2007, p. 12). Such scripts can limit women, for example, as victims or as powerful. The discourses of religion, gender and sexuality and nation come together in late modernity:

> It is now clearly established that the West has no privileged claim over modernity, and that there are many possible trajectories. From the stance of many of the people whose worlds this paper describes, a modernity where women's economic and political empowerment is accompanied by their pervasive sexualisation is at least as "paradoxical" as one in which religion is valued. (White 2010, p. 342)

The 'girl power' movement of the 1990s is evidence of a social shift to ascribe women with power, which, harnessed, placed them on a level playing field with other dominant groups. Recent research into young women's agency found that although the ways in which they framed their lives drew from a 'discourse of empowerment', tangible measures of oppression continue to surround women's lives (Baker 2010). The same research found that this action enabled young women to 'claim volition and evade victimhood' (Baker 2010, p. 15). The discourse of 'girl power' has not translated into areas of continuing oppression. This new era points to a difficulty in separating agency from structure because of inherent complexities resulting from the current historical period:

> First modernity reflexivity was a matter of reflection. Indeed Habermas's communicative action might be paradigmatic, of not reflexive but "*reflective* modernization*". Second modernity reflexivity is about the emergent demise of the distinction between structure and agency altogether. It is not about reflection at all. (Lash 2003, p. 50–51)

At the same time material differences continue to exist in the experiences of men and women in society (Skeggs 1997). Women continue to be the largest group directly affected by sexual violence throughout childhood and adulthood. For same-sex attracted women, that risk increases (Martin et al. 2011). Women are overrepresented in diagnoses of mental illnesses such as depression and black women are more likely to be institutionalised in mental health facilities than their white counterparts. Despite the claims of new forms of gender relationships, research shows that interactions reveal an embedded sexual script which draws from traditional gender norms (Dworking and O'Sullivan 2007).

Whilst late modernity has brought with it many tangible changes to the landscape, such as the use of technology in everyday life, it is true to say that we face ongoing challenges and increased complexities when understanding oppression and inequality. This is because with the fragmentation of social life (Elliott 2001), multiple – and contradictory – discourses co-exist (Jackson 2007). In understanding how to respond to these complexities in social work, some of the theoretical traditions which have been explored in this chapter include Foucault, the work of George Herbert Mead, as well as theorists of late modernity. Whereas power can be understood through a historical-social Foucauldian approach, so too can it help to understand the tensions between agency and structure. Mead's self, which we examined in Chapter 3 of this book, helps to understand this through sociality and biography: "the idea of the social self, originating from the work of Mead, provides a view of the self as social while allowing for agency through the emphasis on interpretive practices" (Jackson and Scott 2011, p. 94). Here the idea of the social self is helpful and locates meaning at the individual or micro level. As McNay notes:

> …in order to avoid an absolutization of the subject, any theory of agency must be placed within the context of overarching material and symbolic constraints. However, at the same time, these deterministic tendencies need to be counterbalanced by a hermeneutic understanding of the process of self-formation. (McNay 2000, p. 80)

In this chapter we have argued that late modern social work involves a greater requirement to understand the space and time dimensions to practice. This involves social work's engagement with sociological theories about temporality and spatiality. There is some work in this area in social work literature (see, for example, Ferguson 2002; 2008; 2011) and, no doubt, more scholarship will emerge in coming years. Theories of time and space help to ground social work and understanding these concepts provides social workers with new ways to understand the influence of their environment upon the work that they undertake with others.

Further Reading

Adkins, L. (2002) *Revisions: Gender and Sexuality in Late Modernity*, Buckingham: Open University Press.

Ferguson, H. (2008) Liquid Social Work: Welfare Interventions as Mobile Practices, *British Journal of Social Work*, 38, pp. 561–79.

Ferguson, H. (2011) *Child Protection Practice*, Basingstoke, Palgrave McMillan.

Ferguson, H. and Powell, F.W. (2002) Social Work in Late-Modern Ireland, in *Social Work in the British Isles*, edited by Payne, M. and Shardlow, S., London: Jessica Kingsley.

Heaphy, B. (2007) *Late Modernity and Social Change: Reconstructing Social and Personal Life*, Abingdon: Routledge.

Mead, G.H. (1929) The Nature of the Past, in *G.H. Mead: A Reader*, edited by Silva, F.C., London: Routledge.

Chapter 10
Social Work and Capitalism

Introduction

Social work in advanced industrialised nations takes place within capitalist social structures. In this context, a capitalist economic system is the prevailing economic order; the dominant means of production and distribution of goods and service, and source of paid labour. Further, it is a reference for the public policies and policy implementation of governmental systems, including fiscal and monetary policies. Despite persistent counter narratives for the 'social' to be at the heart of a society, argued for by many social workers over time (Mowbray 1985; Mullaly 1997; Dominelli 1997; Houston 2010; Garrett 2013), the continuing hegemony is market economics, and the requirements for fiscal surplus or balance, endorsed credit ratings, economic growth and company profits. The austerity policies of European governments are predicated on this logic. We see this each and every night on the news with finance reports showing these indicators as purportedly the signs of the health of the nation. This capitalist market economic dominance has relevance to social work in many kaleidoscopic ways. It is the focus of discussion in this chapter.

Social Work and the Market

Social workers work alongside, and with, people, families, communities and broader social associations that interact with social workers, in some measure, because of their economic circumstances. This may be owing to a person being on a low income and without sufficient material resources to meet their needs, on pensions and benefits and in contact, therefore, with a social welfare or security system. There are also many people in these situations that will never need or want to see social workers, or will do so for other reasons beyond material issues. As welfare states have become more conditional and residual, there has been an increase in tighter surveillance of payment beneficiaries (Bryson and Verity 2009). Sheila Shaver, a social policy writer, calls this 'a shift from sovereignty to supervision' (2001, p. 1), a dynamic in which social work is implicated.

As well as the above, the capitalist market economic dominance has important relevance because of the income and wealth inequalities that arise through market economics. There is a constant stream of reports that continue to reveal the extent of this inequality and how gaps are widening, not closing.

Numerous reports analysing data from the UK show the extent of income and wealth inequality in the country, and how it manifests in the lives of different social groups. The gap between rich and poor continues to rise (OECD 2008; Centre for Analysis of Social Exclusion 2010; Rowlingson 2012) and is winding back the clock on the gains of the post war welfare state and the promise of social justice. The gap is geographic or locationally defined, but income and wealth inequalities are also based in gender, race, life-stage and health status. In a study of wealth inequality, Rowlingson found that 'the distribution of wealth is highly unequal with the top 10 per cent owning 100 times more than the bottom 10 percent' (2012, p. 3). The OECD, in a 2008 report on inequality, noted that; '…the gap between the rich and poor is still greater in the UK than in three quarters of OECD countries' (2008, p. 1). Similar patterns of rising inequality are to be found within many countries across the world, and there are disturbing patterns of inequalities between nations (Castells 1998; Bauman 1998) in the context of the faceless and unaccountable nature of global capital. On this matter Zygmunt Bauman writes:

> The mobility required by "people who invest" – those with capital, with money which the investment requires – means the new, indeed unprecedented in its radical unconditionality, disconnection of power from obligations: duties towards employees, but also towards the younger and weaker, towards yet unborn generations and towards the self-reproduction of living conditions of all; in short, freedom from the duty to contribute to daily life and the perpetuation of the community. There is a new asymmetry emerging between exterritorial nature of power and the continuing territoriality of the "whole life" – which the now unanchored power, able to move at short motive and without warning, is free to exploit and abandon the consequences of that exploitation. (Bauman 1998, p. 9)

The Australian Government Social Inclusion Unit produces a report called 'How is Australia Faring'. Headlines from the *Second Report* (2012) include: 'Lone parent families continue to have the highest levels of financial stress' and 'Income inequality remains higher than it was in the mid 1990s' and 'The gap between low and middle income groups remains' and 'Women have higher rates of persistent low economic resources' (http://www.socialinclusion.gov.au/resources/financial-stress-and-inequality).

In 2005 the *First Report of Australian Social Attitudes* was released. This is a study based on survey responses from 4,270 Australians who were asked their views and attitudes on a number of areas. A survey finding is, that whilst respondents knew that there has been rising inequality in Australia, such as wages and profits of the insurance and banking sectors, and were troubled by it, they were not, however, enthusiastic about redistributing income and wealth to 'ordinary working people' (2005, p. 175). Sociological social work can aid in understanding why the New Right's ideas about 'welfare dependency', why self interests in the context of individualism have such a strong hold and why there is such an embedded cultural resistance to wealth redistribution. A recent text by Owen Jones (2011), for example, argues that various historical and social forces such as post industrial geographical shifts as well as a dominant market ideology have aligned to 'demonise' the working class.

Neo-liberal Organisational Architecture

The workings of a market economic social structure are relevant for social work because of the dominance of neo-liberalism throughout the workings of the state. Workers operate from institutional contexts that are part of a deepening, and more fragmented, neo-liberal welfare state with a continuing trend of individualising service agendas. The ideas that shape organisations, as discussed earlier, are based in market ideas and practices that have been imported into the social service systems. This is an ill fit. Much of the social work critical debate about the characteristics of contemporary life have been summarised through a questioning of neo-liberalist ideology. Competition, dominance of capital and finance and the overarching emphasis on the individual: all of these are associated with neo-liberalism and ought to be understood as such in social work (Garrett 2013, p. 82–4). As we discussed in Chapter 5, decisions made through legislation, social policy and organisational policies and practices affect the ways in which social workers practice and potentially cause ethical ambiguities and clashes. In short: broader changes to society impact upon the nature of social work itself.

Neo-liberal inputs have included the use of the language and terms of the capitalist market. These days it is not unusual for human service agencies to have procedures and documents wherein is a language that the people with whom they have contact are called 'customers' or 'consumers', and to be engaged in business planning and other market based practices, even if these are resisted by the social workers themselves. The language we use is never value free or neutral (Plant 1970; Bryson 1992; Williams 1999). The dictionary definition of 'customer' tells us that they are 'a person who purchases goods or services from another; a buyer; a patron' (Macquarie 2006, p. 295). The application of the term 'customer' to social work practice signals a very different relationship; such an association of a consumer in a market exchange is not a social work relationship, and the use of this language obfuscates power inequalities in the relationship and the conditions upon which people come to need social work assistance. For example the inequalities referred to earlier in Chapter 7 in relation to climate change. The language of consumer or customer implies the ability to exit, or go somewhere else to obtain a service and product, which is called consumer sovereignty in market terms. This is often not the case. How literate are social workers and organisations about the capitalist market? How do we think about the implications and framing implied in the language we are asked to use?

We suggest these to be important questions in social work since there are many instances of ways in which a market rationale is used in service provision. Another example is the increasing need for non-governmental organisations to be required to submit tenders for short-term funding arrangements. The outcome of these tenders, which are competitively applied for and selectively awarded, determine whether or not a particular service continues. In Chapter 5 we explored the ways in which ethical choices made at broader levels impacted service provision in social work. Similarly, the outsourcing of particular services brings about concerns about the ethical appropriateness of services being run by whichever organisation is prepared to offer the lowest costs to win a competitive tender for services. Is it, for example, fitting for some social services to be run by for-profit companies? In the following quote, the language of a market model of service delivery is evident:

> Our business developed as a result of the outsourcing of government services during the 1990s in the search for innovative funding and management solutions to increasingly complex problems. We operate to the highest standards in meeting both government and community expectations and often surpass the performance of comparable government operated facilities. (GSL)

This quote comes from Global Solutions Limited Australia (GSL Australia) which is a company that has held a contract to manage detention centres for asylum seekers and refugees.

The rise of insurance issues in social work is another example of the application of market ideology, policy and practices which relate to the assessment of risk and consideration of its financial equivalence. Beck, in his work on risk societies, introduces an image of insurance companies having a prescient gaze on the unfolding social world. He notes, 'It is the private insurance companies which patrol the frontier of risk society' (Beck 2009, p. 110). In the wake of extreme weather events and the impacts of them, we read in the media, and with increasing regularity, about insurance.[1] Questions are raised about who, and in what combination, should be responsible for covering the losses incurred in extreme weather events – governments, private insurance companies, civil society through philanthropy, or citizens through their own funds or additional tax

---

1 See, for example, *The Australian,* 6 March 2011.

measures like 'Flood Levies'? Insurance is to a policy holder sold as 'protection' against harm and loss, both in a financial sense, but also at a level that insurers sell as reassurance. The Australian Securities Investment Commission in an insurance fact sheet succinctly puts it: 'Insurance protects you from financial loss when things go wrong' (2008, p. 39). They also explain that insurance is 'transferring the risk of having to pay – if something goes wrong – to the *insurer*' (2008, p. 39). Private insurance is however more than this; it is intricate in the workings of global capital and as such a source of power (Elliott 2003, p. 31). The complete workings of the insurance market from anticipation and calculation of risk probabilities, what Ulrich Beck calls the 'attempt to anticipate the worst possible turn' (2009, p. 129), the terms and conditions of claim payouts, product disclosure and the inter relationships with individual and organisational risk management; these are all contested in dynamics of power relations.

In the Australian context, civil society has felt the impact of what happens when insurance costs rise (Verity 2012). In 2001, a large company called HIH Insurance Group collapsed, and with it went capital investments and financial futures; it furthermore impacted heavily on certain sectors like the building sector (Owen 2003). Locating affordable insurance, especially public liability insurance, became a pressing matter for civil society organisations. This has been noted as detrimental in its own terms (Senate Economics Reference Committee 2002; Verity 2006), but also in respect to unintended consequences, such as organisational time spent on risk management, the elevation of a culture of 'risk as fear' rather than 'risk as promise' and practices of risk avoidance. The HIH Inquiry Royal Commissioner Owen also points to how '[A]...collapse of this magnitude must inevitably shake public confidence in the insurance industry and in the regulatory system's ability to carry out its protective role properly' (2003, p.16).

The Counsel assisting the Commission, Hon. Wayne Martin, writing in 2007 on this matter of the collapse of HIH uses the analogy that 'a fish rots from the head' to make the point that the trappings of governance and risk management were in place within the company but that company leaders focused on what they could get away with 'not what was morally or ethically "right"' (Australian Institute of Company Director 2007, p. 4–5). This echoes Bauman's comments about the disconnection between economic agendas and a social responsibility. The collapse of HIH also resulted in large government bailouts of which Harold Luntz, a prominent Australian law scholar, writes:

> Despite the current Federal Government's ideological opposition to interference with market forces, it stepped in…The Parliament appropriated A\$640 million to meet claims arising out of the collapse of the HIH Group of companies… The ultimate cost to taxpayers is likely to run into hundreds of millions of dollars. (Luntz 2004, p. 889)

In a market model which is central in a private market insurance context, consumer sovereignty is a principle. Yet many not-for-profit organisations are provided with contracts for funds that tell them what insurance they must have and the cover required. In the face of these practices how sustainable is this investment in insurance? More to the point what is private insurance purchased for and how does it relate to risk management conducted within the organisation? If insurance is to remain a private matter, that is, not covered through government insurance schemes, is it not prudent for civil society organisations to be active and educated insurance consumers?

Sociological Social Work in Late Capitalist Society

Sociological social work involves the adoption of established and emerging theories from sociology which help to understand and situate social work practice and theory:

> Classical and contemporary Euro-American social theory took shape in no small measure as a theoretical reckoning with industrial capitalism. Whether we consider Marx's critique of political economy, Durkheim's analysis of the social division of labor or Weber's thesis of the Protestant origins of the disciplining of capital and labor, these thinkers aimed to explain the development of industrial capitalism – its political economy, class system, patterns of solidarity, and link to bureaucratization and state formation. A century later, "capitalism", now understood as an information-based global economy, remains a central focus of social theory and politics. (Seidman 2013, p. 3)

Neo-liberalism has been cited as the ideological basis for the reorientation towards the individual and, alongside institutional reflexivity (Giddens 1991) has changed the ways in which individuals relate to one another in institutional forms. Lash argues that although forms of relating have changed, the process of individualization is far from linear. In this project:

> Lash looks to Germany and Japan for examples of reflexive production and in particular to demonstrate the significance of "pre-modern", traditional forms in these regimes. He shows that promotion incentives in large firms in Japan are often tightly linked to the acquisition of knowledge or information, and that flows of information are optimized through personalized trust relations. Thus employment contracting is often "relational" where exchange relationships involve not only straightforwardly cash-nexus exhanges but also symbolic exchanges, for example, of shared identities. (Adkins 2002, p. 34)

Awareness of other nations and economies can help in critiquing local and international systems and practices. The Global Economic Crisis (GEC) has massively influenced so many people including governments and citizens in Europe, the United States of America and many other countries to varying degrees. One of the outcomes from the GEC is that there has been increased reflection about market-driven values. Marx's work is often used in analyses of capitalism. Marx has been argued as relevant to social work in contemporary times, but this is not a simple application, rather, Marx's ideas ought to be extended toward the complex contours of our late modern landscape:

> To social workers committed to such an endeavour, Marxist analysis offers an indispensable counter-hegemonic perspective on our neoliberal times. Capitalism is deeply fissured through its own internal contradictions. There is, therefore, a pressing need for an analysis of these contradictions and this requires the deployment of theoretical tools such as those that Marx pioneered. The task is not to regurgitate Marx's texts, but to extend, revise and adapt them in ways that can address the complexities of our times. (Garrett 2013, p. 63)

Garrrett also notes that Marx is used as a 'useful resource for a more politically alert, activist, anti-capitalist form of social work' (Garrett 2013, p. 74) and cites Lavalette's work as particularly relevant to this cause (Lavalette 2011). Yet Marx's ideas can help frame mainstream social work too. Heightening awareness about modes of production, power and labour all help to better understand interpersonal and political dynamics. We argue that social workers must firstly remain aware about the language and culture of neo-liberalism and capitalism in their everyday work experiences. Secondly, social workers need to highlight the disjunction between market ideology and social work theory and practice while actively working to promote the values and ethics intrinsic to our profession. Taking a perspective which sees the dominance of capitalism as a historical phenomenon helps to highlight some of the innovative and optimistic developments in which communities and nations and global citizens have come together in the wake of the GEC. Social work's history of working in communities does much to legitimise the continuing need for the profession to promote the role of understanding the individual in their social, cultural, global and *historical* context.

Recommended Reading

Fine, B. and Saad-Filho, A. (2004) *Marx's Capital*, Pluto Press: London.
Harvey, D. (2005) *A Brief History of Neoliberalism*, Oxford University Press: Oxford.
Wood, E. (2002) *The Origin of Capitalism: A Longer Term View*, Verso: London.
McClelland, D. (1974) *Karl Marx: His Life and Thought*, London: Macmillan.

Chapter 11
Conclusions for Sociological Social Work in a Changing World

In *Sociological Social Work* we have examined what sociological social work requires and what it means to social work scholarship, practice and education. We have argued that firstly, social workers require the desire to adopt a sociological sensibility and the curiosity this implies. Using the work of sociologists such as C. Wright Mills, and in line with a social work tradition, we have argued that social workers' imaginations must extend beyond the individual, into the social worlds around them, and back. This imagination includes the natural world. Secondly, we have argued that increased awareness of, and engagement in, theories which examine selfhood help social workers and the social work profession to critically engage with its own values, ideas and purpose, is required. In Chapter 3 we argued that social workers must be congruent in their professional identities and their personal or day-to-day selves.

Yet there is another requirement for a way of working which is named as sociological social work. This requirement is integral to this project. Social workers wishing to work in a way which can be described as sociological social work require literacy in sociological and social work theories, and a way to hold these in an integral whole. We have critically examined some of the key ideas in sociology and explored how these help one to better understand and interpret the world around us throughout this book. We have explored, for example, the tensions which arise in organisational settings and in practice situations and how thinking sociologically can assist in delving deeper into the relations at work in certain fields.

The common thread that joins up what can seem like endless sociological theories has been an interest in the ways in which individuals, groups and communities come together. In this *coming together*, the fluidity of the social act is evident: interaction occurs across time and space. Interactions are both replications of patterns of behaviour and social positions, and for scholars such as George Herbert Mead, constitutive or generative of selfhood. In Mead's theory of self, so powerful is sociality, or social interaction, that it generates the self. Similarly, Harriet Bartlett argues that integrative practices uniquely tie us to one another. Pierre Bourdieu's habitus and field remind us of the relationship between individual practices and habits and the ways in which they form a symbiosis with the space they inhabit. All of these ideas speak to the human requirement for interaction. Interaction is the foundation upon which social workers develop positive relationships with those around them, including colleagues and clients.

Yet, as we have seen, the world is changing. Shifts in economic, geographical, environmental and governmental contexts affect social, cultural and political contexts. Day-to-day life for the individual both reflects and influences these broader shifts, as we have seen throughout this book. We have identified some of the major drivers of change; the rise of digital technological innovations; economic, industrial or occupational changes and environmental change. All of the developments in these areas alter the ways in which we interact. In Chapter 9 we considered the ways in which social work is practised in late modern space and time, and began to unravel some of the complexities associated with this task that is situated in the context of global capitalism.

It is true to say that the world is changing and the ways in which individuals relate to one another is changing. Just as with the invention of the telephone, new forms of relating are emerging. Person-to-technology interactions can connect people with others, but there is technology at the interface of such connections. Social work is beginning to think through the ways in which itself as a profession needs to adapt to these altered patterns of interaction (see, for example, Ferguson 2008), but more work is required in this area in relation to theory, research and practice. Though practitioners may already adapt technologies to assist in their work with clients, it is not always the focus of social work scholarship and research.

We have argued that it is important that social workers engage with their changing world, however at the same time, social work cannot be distracted into unthinkingly adopting discourses associated with the contemporary world. One example of this is the ways in which notions of risk have been used to limit social work interventions through the usage of insurance-industry defined rationale. Social workers need to take risks to work for justice, and to speak out about social needs and hopes is as much a needed task. A further example is the pervasive nature of neo-liberalism which has and continues to remake so many aspects of institutional life and the settings and contracts of social relations between the state and citizen. In Chapter 8 we opened a window on time in social work, and used the sociological ideas of Barbara Adam and Manuel Castells to think about temporality and social relations and expectations in the changing world.

Given the complexities involved in social work practice in late modernity or our contemporary world, how is it that we can remain focussed and retain our sociological lens? At the beginning of this book we explored the use of the kaleidoscope metaphor to represent sociological social work. Let us now return to this image. David Brewster, who patented the kaleidoscope, described it as a 'new optical instrument, for creating and exhibiting beautiful forms, is derived from the Greek words beautiful, a form and to see' (1858, p. 1). Viewing the world through the kaleidoscope places a distance between the individual and what is viewed. In this way, the kaleidoscope enables a tangible distance in which what is seen can be analysed using sociological theories. The use of such theories momentarily separates the individual from society and place; both of these within a historical and social context. In this temporal space, the social worker must bring together time and space, and social and historical contexts, alongside the individual and their biography. This is the point at which sociological social work takes place: the application of sociological theory alongside social work theory translates into practice. Sociological social work is both informed by theory but crucially, is manifest in the everyday micro interactions between a social worker and their client(s).

In this book we have built and demonstrated an approach to sociological social work by using existing work in which sociology has been used in social work (Dominelli 1997; Cunningham and Cunningham 2008). These approaches argue that sociology helps to understand and frame people's problems and social issues and institutions, by drawing out a better appreciation of the world through the application of sociological theory. We agree that this is vital but also contend that sociological social work ought to be discernible in the interactions between social workers and the people with whom they work. The purpose of this is to convey how sociological social work might be envisaged in practice. It is not enough that social workers understand sociology: sociology ought to be shared with our clients/community groups we work with and to frame our work. Although this may appear at first glance as something new, as we have seen in Chapter 1, sociology and social work were partners early on in social work's development. Since this time, there has been some work which has developed the cause for a more sociological lens to be used in understanding social work (Dominelli 1997; Ife 1997).

Yet sociological social work needs to be developed and understood on its own terms as an approach in social work. In this project it is useful to understand the ways in which psychological discourses and ways of viewing the world have already been adapted in much of our work. The ways that social work views individuals is very much influenced by psychological discourses which locate the mind within the conscious and unconscious; an idea which draws from psychoanalytic theory. As we have discussed in *Sociological Social Work*, there are other models of selfhood which reject this idea. The language we use to inform and describe our work overlaps with models in health, psychology and other disciplines informed by the pure sciences: we 'intervene' and believe that childhood is a predictor of adult behaviour because identity is formed in the early years. Social work takes on this knowledge unthinkingly, just as psychological discourses of the self have been accepted into popular culture (Furedi 2004; Lasch 1979). Whilst some theories and approaches which originate from psychology may indeed assist us in achieving social justice and responding to client need, a more critical application of this knowledge ought to occur in social work. Uncritically accepting these 'truths' is to the detriment of the social lens. It is important that psychological ways of seeing the world do not act as an elastic band which holds us back. Sociological social work requires familiarity with the key paradigms in sociology as well as the new and emerging theories which help explain our social worlds.

Whereas our vision of a sociological social work can be seen as too invested in theory, we have argued that the contents of the kaleidoscope must be held together by the presence of the commitment to social justice. In Chapter 5 we argued that everyday ethics are crucial to consider in the development of the social work self. We also argued that social justice ought to inform all of our work with others and be present in the social work interaction. Whereas the ethical dimension to social work in late modernity can tip us into a realm underpinned by rationality and neo-liberal values, actively addressing inequality ought to be the ethical foundation upon which our work is constructed. This focus helps to better equip social workers to respond to the challenges faced in contemporary practice settings, including the challenges brought about through organisational restraints as well as organisational freedoms.

Yet what is the future of social work and how does sociological social work assist in responding positively to the challenges brought about by the changes in contemporary life? We contend that in looking through the kaleidoscope which represents sociological social work, social workers must work to connect individuals with the world around them. There is an exciting movement towards a global social work agenda (see http://ifsw.org/get-involved/agenda-for-social-work/) and a global value base informing social work (Ife 2008). The adaptation of the global into social work purpose helps to pull people together toward a common purpose which hinges on our connection to one another and the world around us – social solidarity. Such movements are important to nurture, not least because they stand against individualising movements and interpretations of our current world. Sociological social work is framed around a particular type of knowledge, which has developed through a dominant westernised ontology. Adapting to the global stage involves embracing, questioning and unlearning some of our core assumptions: this is not possible without a sociological imagination or sensibility, literacy in sociology and social work and a commitment to the reduction of oppression, inequality and injustice.

References

ACOSS. (2011) *Community Services Sector Survey for 2011*, Sydney: Australian Council of Social Service.

Adam, B. (1990) *Time and Social Theory*, Cambridge: Polity Press in association with Blackwell Publishing.

Adam, B. (2004) *Time*, Cambridge: Polity Press.

Adams, M. (2003) 'The Reflexive Self and Culture: A Critique', *The British Journal of Sociology*, 54(2), pp. 221–38.

Adkins, L. (2002) *Revisions: Gender and Sexuality in Late Modernity*, Buckingham: Open University Press.

Adkins, L. (2003) 'Reflexivity: Freedom or habit of gender?', *Theory, Culture & Society*, 20, pp. 21–42.

Alexander, J.C. (1996) 'Critical Reflections on "Reflexive Modernization"', *Theory, Culture & Society*, 13(4), pp. 133–8.

Alford, J. and O'Neill, D. (1994) *The Contract State: Public Management and the Kennett Government*, Geelong: Centre for Applied Social Research.

Arches, J. (1991) 'Social Structure, Burnout and Job Satisfaction', *Social Work*, 36(3), pp. 202–6.

Arendt, H. (1969) 'On Violence', in *Crises of the Republic*, edited by Arendt, H., Florida: Harcourt Brace and Company.

Argyris, C. and Schön, D.A. (1974) *Theory in Practice: Increasing Professional Effectiveness*, 1st edn, San Francisco: Jossey-Bass Publishers.

Australian Broadcasting Commission (1945) *The Community Can Do It: Make a Plan*, Sydney: F.H. Booth and Sons.

Australian Bureau of Statistics (2008) *Water and the Murray-Darling Basin*, Canberra: Australian Bureau of Statistics.

Australian Bureau of Statistics (2013) *Internet Activity, Australia, December 2012*, Canberra: Australian Bureau of Statistics.

Banks, S. (2003) *Ethics and Values in Social Work*, Basingstoke: Palgrave Macmillan.

Bartlett, H. (1970) *The Common Base of Social Work Practice*, USA: National Association of Social Workers.

Bauman, Z. (1990) *Thinking Sociologically*, Oxford: Blackwell.

Bauman, Z. (1993) *Postmodern Ethics*, Oxford: Blackwell.

Bauman, Z. (1998) *Globalization: The Human Consequences*, Cambridge: Polity Press.

Bauman, Z. (2000) *Liquid Modernity*, Cambridge: Polity Press.

Bauman, Z. (2001) *Community. Seeking Safety in an Insecure World*, Cambridge: Polity Press.

Bauman, Z. (2003) *Liquid Love: on the Frailty of Human Bonds*, Cambridge: Polity Press.

Bauman, Z. and May, T. (2001) *Thinking Sociologically*, Oxford: Blackwell Publishing.

Beauchamp, T.L. and Childress, J.F. (1989) *Principles of Biomedical Ethics*, 2nd edn, New York: Oxford University Press.

Beck, U. (1992) *Risk Society: Towards a New Modernity*, London: Sage.

Beck, U. (1994) 'The Re-Invention of Politics: Towards a New Theory of Reflexive Modernization', in *Reflexive Modernization: Politics, Tradition and Aesthetics in the Modern Social Order*, edited by Beck, U., Giddens, A. and Lash, S., Cambridge: Polity Press.

Beck, U. and Beck-Gernsheim, E. (2001) *Individualization*, London: Sage.

Beck, U. (2009) *World at Risk*, Cambridge: Polity Press.

Beers, S. and De Bellis, M. (2002) 'Neuropsychological function in children with maltreatment-related post-traumatic stress disorder', *American Journal of Psychiatry*, 159(3), pp. 483–7.

Berger, J. (1977) *Ways of Seeing*, London: Penguin Books.

Berger, P. and Luckmann, T. (1967) *The Social Construction of Reality: a Treatise in the Sociology of Knowledge*, London: Allen Lane.

Blokland, T. (2003) *Urban Bonds: Social Relationships in an Inner City Neighbourhood*, Cambridge: Polity Press.

Bourdieu, P. (1977) *Outline of a Theory of Practice*, Cambridge: Cambridge University Press.

Bourdieu, P. (1984) *Distinction*, London: Routledge and Kegan Paul.

Bourdieu, P. (1991) *Language and Symbolic Power*, Cambridge, MA: Harvard University Press.

Bourdieu, P. and Wacquant, L.J.D. (1992) *An Invitation to Reflexive Sociology*, Chicago: University of Chicago Press.

Bowles, W., Collingridge, M., Curry, S. and Valentine, B. (2006) *Ethical Practice in Social Work: An Applied Approach*, Crows Nest: Allen and Unwin.

Breaking New Ground. (2012) *Submission to: Review of Not-For-Profit Governance Arrangements*, NSW: Breaking New Ground.

Bryson, L., and Mowbray, M. (1981) '"Community": The Spray-On Solution', *Australian Journal of Social Issues*, 16(4), pp. 255–67.

Bryson, L. (1992) *Welfare and the State: Who Benefits?*, London: Macmillan Press.

Burkitt, I. (1994) 'The Shifting Concept of the Self', *History of the Human Sciences*, 7(2), pp. 7–28.

Büscher, M. and Urry, J. (2009) 'Mobile Methods and the Empirical', *European Journal of Social Theory*, 12(1), pp. 99–116.

REFERENCES

Butler, J. (1990) *Gender Trouble: Feminism and the Subversion of Gender,* London: Routledge.

Carey, M. and Foster, V. (2011) 'Introducing "Deviant" Social Work: Contextualising the Limits of Radical Social Work whilst Understanding (Fragmented) Resistance within the Social Work Labour Process', *British Journal of Social Work,* 41(3), pp. 576–93.

Carson, E. and Kerr, L. (2010) 'Contractualism, workforce development and sustainability in the community services sector', *Third Sector Review,* 16(1), pp. 69–87.

Castells, M. (1989) *The Informational City: Information Technology, Economic Restructuring and the Urban-Regional Process,* Oxford: Blackwell Publishers Inc.

Castells, M. (1996) *The Rise of the Network Society,* Malden MA: Blackwell Publishers Inc.

Castells, M. (1997) *The Power of Identity,* Massachusetts, USA: Blackwell Publishers Inc.

Castells, M. (1998) *End of Millennium – The Information Age: Economy, Society and Culture Volume III,* Malden MA: Blackwell Publishers Inc.

Chaskin, R. (1997) 'Perspectives on neighborhood and community: a review of the literature', *Social Service Review,* 71(4), pp. 521–47

Cheek, J. (1996) *Society and Health: Social Theory for Health Workers,* Melbourne: Longman Australia.

Clarke, J. (2004) 'Dissolving the Public Realm?: The logics and limits of neo-liberalism', *Journal of Social Policy,* 33(1), pp. 27–48.

Cleak, H. and Wilson, J. (2004) *Making the Most of Field Placement,* Sydney: Cengage Learning Australia Pty Limited.

Clegg, S. and Baumeler, C. (2010) 'Essai: From iron cages to liquid modernity in organization analysis', *Organization Studies,* 31(12), pp. 1713–33.

Compton, B., and Galaway, B. (1979) *Social Work Processes,* Homewood: The Dorsey Press.

Connell, R. (1987) *Gender and Power: Society, the Person, and Sexual Politics,* Sydney: Allen and Unwin.

Connell, R., and Messerschmidt, J. (2005) 'Hegemonic masculinity: rethinking the concept', *Gender and Society,* 19(6), pp. 829–31.

Considine, M. and Painter, M. (1997) 'Introduction', in *Managerialism: The Great Debate,* edited by Considine, M., and Painter, M., Carlton South: Melbourne University Press, pp. 1–11.

Corrigan, O. (2003) 'Empty ethics: the problem with informed consent', *Sociology of Health & Illness,* 25(7), pp. 768–92.

Coulshed, V. and Mullender, A. (2001) *Management in Social Work,* Basingstoke: Palgrave Macmillan.

Craig, G. (1998) 'Community Development in a Global Context', *Community Development Journal,* 33(1), pp. 2–17.

Crossley, N. (2001) *The Social Body: Habit, Identity and Desire*, London: Thousand Oaks.

Cunningham, J. and Cunningham, S. (2008) *Sociology and Social Work*, Exeter: Learning Matters Ltd.

Delima, J. and Vimpani, G. (2011) 'The neurobiological effects of childhood maltreatment: An often overlooked narrative related to the long-term effects of early childhood trauma?', *Australian Institute of Family Studies*, 89.

Denemark, D., and Niemi, R. (2012) 'Political trust, efficacy and engagement in challenging times: an introduction', *Australian Journal of Political Science*, 47(1), pp. 1–10.

Dominelli, L. (1997) *Sociology for Social Work,* Basingstoke: Palgrave.

Dominelli, L. (2011) 'Climate change: social workers' roles and contributions to policy debates and interventions', *International Journal of Social Welfare*, 20(4), pp. 430–38.

du Gay, P. (1993) '"Numbers and souls": retailing and the de-differentiation of economy and culture', *The British Journal of Sociology,* 44, pp. 563–87.

Dunk-West, P. (2012) 'The Sexual Self and Social Work and Policy, or, Why Teenage Pregnancy Prevention Programmes Miss the Point', *Social Work & Society,* 10(2).

Dunk-West, P. (2011) 'Everyday Sexuality and Identity: De-Differentiating the Sexual Self in Social Work' in *Sexual Identities and Sexuality in Social Work: Research and Reflections from Women in the Field*, edited by Dunk-West, P. and Hafford-Letchfield, T., Farnham: Ashgate.

Dunk-West, P. (2013) *How to be a Social Worker: A Critical Guide for Students,* Basingstoke: Palgrave Macmillan.

Dunk-West, P. (forthcoming) 'Social Work Identity, Power and Selfhood: A Re-imagining' in *Rethinking Anti-Discriminatory Practice, Diversity and Equality in Social Work*, edited by Cocker, C. and Hafford-Letchfield, T., Basingstoke: Palgrave Macmillan.

Dunk, P. (2007) 'Everyday sexuality and Social Work: Locating Sexuality in Profressional Practice and Education', *Social Work and Society* 5(2), pp. 135–42.

Durkheim, E. (1952 [1897]) *Suicide: A Study in Sociology,* London: Routledge and Kegan Paul.

Durkheim, E. (1976 [1912]) *The Elementary Forms of Religious Life,* London: Allen and Unwin.

Durkheim, E. (1982 [1895]) *The Rules of Sociological Method,* London: Macmillan.

Durkheim, E. (1984 [1893]) *The Division of Labour in Society,* London: Macmillan.

Emirbayer, M. and Williams, E. (2005) 'Bourdieu and Social Work', *Social Service Review*, 79, pp. 689–724.

Erikson, E. (1950) *Childhood and Society*, New York: Norton.

Etzioni, A. (1996) *The New Golden Rule: Community and Morality in a Democratic Society*, New York: Basic Books.

Etzioni, A. (1980) *A Sociological Reader on Complex Organizations*, New York: Holt, Rinehart and Winston.

Fahlgren, S. (2009) 'Discourse analysis of a childcare drama: Or the interfaces between paradoxical discourses of time in the context of social work', *Time & Society*, 18 (2–3), pp. 208–30.

Ferguson, H. (2001) 'Social Work, Individualization and Life Politics', *British Journal of Social Work*, 31, pp. 41–55.

Ferguson, H. (2008) 'Liquid Social Work: Welfare Interventions as Mobile Practices', *British Journal of Social Work*, 38(3), pp. 561–79.

Ferguson, H. (2009) 'Driven to Care: The Car, Automobility and Social Work', *Mobilities*, 4(2), pp. 275–93.

Ferguson, H. (2011) *Child Protection Practice*, Basingstoke: Palgrave Macmillan.

Ferguson, H. and Powell, F.W. (2002) 'Social Work in Late-Modern Ireland' in *Social Work in the British Isles*, edited by Payne, M. and Shardlow, S., London: Jessica Kingsley.

Fisk, M. (1993) 'Community and Morality' *The Review of Politics*, 54(4), pp. 593–616.

Florida, R. (2008) *Who's your city?: How the creative economy is making where to live the most important decision of your life*, New York: Basic Books.

Fook, J. (1999) 'Critical Reflexivity in Education and Practice' in *Transforming Social Work Practice: Postmodern Critical Perspectives*, edited by Pease, B. and Fook, J., St Leonards: Allen & Unwin.

Forte, J.A. (2004) 'Symbolic Interactionism and Social Work: A Forgotten Legacy, Part 1', *Families in Society*, 85(3), pp. 391–400.

Foucault, M. (1972 [1969]) *The Archaeology of Knowledge*, London: Routledge.

Friedman, M. (1962) *Capitalism and Freedom*, Chicago: University of Chicago Press.

Frontier Economics (2008) *The Diversity of the North: Socio-economic Profiles of the River Basins in the Northern Murray-Darling Basin*, Melbourne: Frontier Economics.

Furedi, F. (2004) *Therapy Culture: Cultivating Vulnerability in an Uncertain Age*, London: Routledge.

Gagnon, J. and Simon, W. (1973) *Sexual Conduct: The Social Sources of Human Sexuality*, Chicago: Aldine.

Gale, P. (2000) *White Australia and Reconciliation: Justice or Just Another Bridge?*, paper presented at the Australian Sociology Association Conference: *Sociological Sites/Sights: Multiple Locations, Multiple Knowledges, Multiple Visions*.

Gambrill, E. (2012) 'Response: Uses of History in Creating New Futures: A Science-Informed Social Work', *Research on Social Work Practice*, 22(5), pp. 481–91.

Gardiner, M. (2004) 'Everyday utopianism', *Cultural Studies*, 18(2/3), pp. 228–54.

Garfinkel, H. (1984) *Studies in Ethnomethodology*, Cambridge: Polity Press.

Garrett, P.M. (2007) 'The Relevance of Bourdieu for Social Work: A Reflection on Obstacles and Omissions', *Journal of Social Work*, 7(3), pp. 355–79.

Garrett, P.M. (2012) 'Re-Enchanting Social Work? The Emerging 'Spirit' of Social Work in an Age of Economic Crisis', *British Journal of Social Work*.

Garrett, P.M. (2013) *Social Work and Social Theory: Making Connections*, Bristol: The Policy Press.

Gauntlett, D. (2007) *Creative Explorations: New Approaches to Identities and Audiences*, London: Routledge.

Gauntlett, D. (2011) *Making is connecting: the social meaning of creativity, from DIY and knitting to YouTube and Web 2.0.*, Cambridge: Polity.

Germov, J., and Williams, L. (1999) *A Sociology of Food and Nutrition: The Social Appetite*, South Melbourne: Oxford University Press.

Giddens, A. (1984) *The Constitution of Society: Outline of the Theory of Structuration*, Berkeley: University of California Press.

Giddens, A. (1989) *Sociology*, Cambridge: Polity Press.

Giddens, A. (1990) *The Consequences of Modernity*, Stanford: Stanford University Press.

Giddens, A. (1991) *Modernity and Self-Identity: Self and Society in the Late Modern Age*, Cambridge: Polity Press.

Giddens, A. (1992) *The Transformation of Intimacy: Sexuality, Love and Eroticism in Modern Societies*, Cambridge: Polity Press.

Giddens, A. (2005) *Sociology*, 4th ed., Cambridge: Polity Press.

Gitterman, A., and Germain, C. (1980) *The Life Model of Social Work Practice*, New York: Columbia University Press.

Goffman, E. (1959) *The Presentation of Self in Everyday Life*, New York: Anchor Books.

Gortmaker, S., Swinburn, B., Levy, D., Carter, R., Mabry, P., Finegood, D., Huang, T., Marsh, T. and Moodie, M. (2011) 'Changing the future of obesity: science, policy and action', *Lancet*, 378, pp. 838–47.

Green, D. and McDermot, F. (2010) 'Social work from inside and between complex systems: perspectives on person-in-environment for today's social work', *British Journal of Social Work*, 40, pp. 2414–30.

Hallett, T. (2003) 'Symbolic Power and Organizational Culture', *Sociological Theory*, 21(2), pp. 128–49.

Hawking, S. (1988) *A Brief History of Time*, New York: Bantam Books.

Healy, K. (2005) *Social Work Theories in Context: Creating Frameworks for Practice*, New York: Palgrave Macmillan.

Holmes, R. (2009) *The Age of Wonder*, London: HarperPress.

Honore, C. (2005) *In Praise of Slow*, London: Orion Books.

Ife, J. (1997) *Rethinking Social Work*, South Melbourne: Addison Wesley Longman Australia Pty Ltd.

Ife, J. (2001) *Human Rights and Social Work: Towards a Rights Based Practice*, Cambridge: Cambridge University Press.

Ife, J. (2008) *Human Rights and Social Work Towards Rights-Based Practice*, Cambridge: Cambridge University Press.

International Bank for Reconstruction and Development. (2012) *Turn Down the Heat: Why a 4 °C Warmer World Must be Avoided*, A Report for the World Bank by the Potsdam Institute for Climate Impact Research and Climate Analytics, Washington: The World Bank.

Jackson, S. (2010) 'Self, Time and Narrative: Re-thinking the Contribution of G.H. Mead', *Life Writing,* 7(2), pp. 123–36.

Jones, A., and May, J. (1992) *Working in Human Service Organisations: A Critical Introduction*, Melbourne: Longman Cheshire

Jones, O. (2011) *Chavs: The Demonisation of the Working Class,* London: Verso.

Kemshall, H. (2002) *Risk, Social Policy and Welfare*, Buckingham: Open University Press.

Kessl, F. (2009) 'Critical reflexivity, social work, and the emerging European post-welfare states', *European Journal of Social Work,* 12(3), pp. 305–17.

Kickbusch, I. (2008) *Adelaide Thinker in Residence Report*, Adelaide: South Australian Government.

Labonte, R. and Laverack, G. (2001a) 'Capacity Building in Health Promotion, Part 1: For Whom? And for what purpose?', *Critical Public Health* 11(2), pp. 111–28.

Lam, C.M., Wong, H. and Leung, T.T.F. (2007) 'An unfinished reflexive journey: social work students' reflection on their placement experiences', *British Journal of Social Work,* 37(1), pp. 91–105.

Lasch, C. (1979) *The Culture of Narcissism: American Life in an Age of Diminishing Expectations,* New York: W.W. Norton.

Lash, S. (2001) 'Technological Forms of Life', *Theory, Culture & Society,* 18(1), pp. 105–20.

Lash, S. (2003) 'Reflexivity as Non-Linearity', *Theory, Culture & Society,* 20(2), pp. 49–57.

Lavalette, M. (2011) *Radical Social Work Today: Social Work at the Crossroads,* Bristol: The Policy Press.

Leaker, M. and Dunk-West, P. (2011) 'Socio-Cultural Risk? Reporting on a Qualitative Study with Female Street-Based Sex Workers', *Sociological Research Online,* 16(4), p. 9.

Lee, J.A.B. (1994) *The Empowerment Approach to Social Work Practice,* New York, USA: Columbia University Press.

Lefebvre, H. (1991) *Critique of Everyday Life: Volume One, Introduction,* London: Verso.

Lemert, C. (2007) *Thinking the Unthinkable: The Riddles of Classical Social Theories,* Boulder, CO: Paradigm Publishers.

Leonard, P. (1966) *Sociology and Social Work,* GB: Nielsen BookScan Product.

Longhofer, J. and Floersch, J. (2012) 'The Coming Crisis in Social Work: Some Thoughts on Social Work and Science', *Research on Social Work Practice,* 22(5), pp. 499–519.

Luntz, H. (2004) 'The Australian Picture' Victorian University Wellington Law Review, 35, pp. 879–903.

Lupton, D. (1997) 'Consumerism, reflexivity and the medical encounter', *Social Science & Medicine,* 45(3), pp. 373–81.

Macey, D. (2009) 'Rethinking biopolitics, race and power in the wake of Foucault', *Theory, Culture and Society,* 26(6), pp. 186–205.

Martin, W. (2007) *People Behaving Badly: Business, politics, football codes and the regulatory response,* Australian Institute of Company Directors WA Division Winter Dinner.

Martinelli, A. (2003) 'Markets, Governments, Communities and Global Governance', *International Sociology,* 18(2), pp. 291–323.

Mayo, E. (1945) *The Social Problems of an Industrial Civilization,* Cambridge, MA: Harvard University Press.

McGuirk, P. and Dowling, R. (2007) 'Understanding master-planned estates in Australian cities: a framework for research', *Urban Policy and Research,* 25(1), pp. 21–38

McLellan, D. (1971) *The Thought of Karl Marx: An Introduction,* New York: Harper and Row.

McMichael, A. and Kovats, R. (2000b) Climate change and climate variability: adaptions to reduce adverse health impacts, *Environmental Monitoring and Assessment,* 61, pp. 49–64.

Mead, G.H. (1908) 'The Philosophical Basis of Ethics' in *G.H. Mead: A Reader,* edited by Silva, F.C., London: Routledge.

Mead, G.H. (1912) 'The Mechanism of Social Consciousness' in *G.H. Mead: A Reader,* edited by Silva, F.C., London: Routledge.

Mead, G.H. (1913) 'The Social Self' in *G.H. Mead: A Reader,* edited by Silva, F.C., Abingdon: Routledge.

Mead, G.H. (1925) 'The Genesis of the Self and Social Control' in *G.H. Mead: A Reader,* edited by Silva, F.C., Abingdon: Routledge.

Mead, G.H. (1929) 'The Nature of the Past' in *G. H. Mead: A Reader,* edited by Silva, F.C., London: Routledge.

Mead, G.H. (1934) *Mind, Self and Society from the Standpoint of a Social Behaviourist,* Chicago: Chicago University Press.

Melucci, A. (1998) 'Inner Time and Social Time in a World of Uncertainty', *Time & Society,* 7(2), pp. 179–91.

Mendes, P. (2003) *Australia's Welfare Wars: The Players, the Politics and the Ideologies,* Sydney: University of New South Wales Press.

Miller, K. and Burns, K. (2008) 'Suicides on farms in South Australia, 1997–2001', *Australian Journal of Rural Health*, 16(6), pp. 327–31.

Mills, C.W. (1959) *The Sociological Imagination,* New York: Oxford University Press.

Monaco, J. (1981) *How to Read a Film: The Art, Technology, Language, History, and Theory of Film and Media,* Oxford: Oxford University Press.

Mowbray, M. (1985) 'The Medicinal Properties of Localism: a Historical Perspective', in *Community Work or Social Change*, edited by Thorpe, R., and Petruchenia, J., London: Routledge and Kegan Paul.

Muetzelfeldt, M. (1994) 'Contracts, Politics and Society', in *The Contract State: public management and the Kennett government*, edited by Alford, J. and O'Neill, D., Geelong: Centre for Applied Social Research.

Mullaly, B. (1997) *Structural Social Work – Ideology, Theory and Practice* (2nd edn), Ontario: Oxford University Press.

Mullaly, B. (1997) *Structural Social Work: Ideology, Theory and Practice,* Ontario: Oxford University Press.

Nayak, A. and Kehily, M.J. (1996) 'Playing it straight: masculinities, homophobias and schooling', *Journal of Gender Studies,* 5(2), pp. 211–30.

Nayak, A. and Kehily, M.J. (2006) 'Gender undone: subversion, regulation and embodiment in the work of Judith Butler', *British Journal of Sociology of Education,* 27(4), pp. 459–72.

Nisbet, R.A. (1966) *The Sociological Tradition,* London: Heinemann Educational Books Ltd.

O'Leary, P., Tsui, M. and Ruch, G. (2012) 'The boundaries of the social work relationship revisited: Towards a connected, inclusive and dynamic conceptualisation', *British Journal of Social Work,* Advanced access, published 10 January 2012 (DOI: 10.1093/bjsw/bcr181).

O'Malley, P. (2004) *Risk, Uncertainty and Government*, London: Glass House Press.

Painter, M. (1997) 'Public Management: Fad or Fallacy?', in *Managerialism: The Great Debate*, edited by Considine, M., and Painter, M., Carlton South: Melbourne University Press.

Payne, M. (2005) *Modern Social Work Theory* (3rd edn), Basingstoke: Palgrave.

Pease, B. (2002) 'Rethinking empowerment: A postmodern reappraisal for emancipatory practice', *British Journal of Social Work,* 32, pp. 135–47.

Perrow, C. (1986) *Complex Organizations: A Critical Essay*, New York: Random House.

Plant, R. (1974) *Community and Ideology*, London: Routledge and Kegan Paul.

Powers, M. (2004) *The Risk Management of Everything: Rethinking The Politics of Uncertainty*, London: Demos.

Productivity Commission (2010) *Contribution of the Not-for-Profit Sector*, Canberra: Productivity Commission.

Pumphrey, R.E. and Pumphrey, M.W. (1961) *The Heritage of American Social Work,* New York: Columbia University Press.

Pusey, M. and Turnbull, N. (2005) 'Have Australians Embraced Economic Reform?', in *Australian Social Attitudes: The First Report*, edited by Wilson, S., Meagher, G., Gibson, R., Denemark, D. and Western, M., Sydney: University of New South Wales Press.

Putnam, R. (2007) 'E Pluribus Unum: Diversity and Community in the Twenty-First Century', *Scandinavian Political Studies*, 30(2), pp. 137–74.

Putnam, R. (undated) *Social Capital: Measurement and Consequences* (accessed at http://www.visionaryvalues.com/wiki/images/Putnam_SocialCapital.pdf).

Reamer, F. (1993) *The Philosophical Foundations of Social Work*, New York: Columbia University Press.

Rittel, H., and Webber, M. (1977) 'Where Models Fail-Dilemmas in a General Theory of Planning', in *Planning for Social Welfare: Issues, Models and Tasks*, edited by Gilbert, N. and Specht, H., New Jersey: Prentice Hall.

Rogers, C. (1961) *On Becoming a Person*, London: Constable & Company.

Rowlingson, K. (2012) *Wealth Inequality: Key Facts*, Birmingham Policy Commissions: Birmingham University.

Sallaz, J. (2010) 'Service Labor and Symbolic Power: on putting Bourdieu to work', *Work and Occupations*, 37(3), pp. 295–319.

Saunders, H. (2005) *Politics is about Relationship: a Blueprint for the Citizens' Century*, New York: Palgrave Macmillan.

Saunders, P. (2004) *Kicking the Welfare Habit*, Sydney: Duffy and Snellgrove.

Schön, D.A. (1983) *The Reflective Practitioner: How Professionals Think in Action*, New York: Basic Books.

Schwartz, W. (1974) 'Private Troubles and Public Issues: One Social Work Job or Two?', in *The Practice of Social Work*, edited by Klenk, R.W. and Ryan, R.W., Belmont: Wadsworth.

Seidman, S. (2013) 'Defilement and disgust: Theorizing the other', *AJCS*, 1(1), pp. 3–25.

Selznick, P. (1948) 'Foundations of the Theory of Organisations', *American Sociological Review*, 13, pp. 25–35.

Shaver, S. (2001) 'Australian Welfare Reform: From Sovereignty to Supervision', *TASA 2001 Conference, The University of Sydney, 13–15 December 2001*, pp. 1–11

Silverman, D. (1970) *The Theory of Organisations*, London: Heinemann.

Singer, P. (2004) *One World: the Ethics of Globalisation*, Melbourne: Text Publishing.

Singer, P. (2009) *The Life You Can Save: Acting Now to End World Poverty*, New York: Random House.

Skeggs, B. (2004) *Class, Self, Culture*, London: Routledge.

Smith, C. (2002) 'The Sequestration of Experience: Rights Talk and Moral Thinking in "Late Modernity"', *Sociology*, 36(1), pp. 43–66.

Solomon, S. (2007) *Climate Change 2007 - The Physical Science Basis: Working Group I Contribution to the Fourth Assessment Report of the IPCC*, New York, USA: Cambridge University Press.

Thorpe, R. (1985) 'Community work and ideology: an Australian perspective', in *Community Work or Social Change? An Australian perspective*, edited by Thorpe, R. and Petruchenia, J., Melbourne: Routledge and Kegan Paul, pp. 11–27.

Titmuss, R. (1969) *Essays on 'The welfare state'*, Boston: Beacon Press.

Tönnies, F. (1971) *On Sociology: Pure, Applied, and Empirical*, edited by Cahnman, Werner and Heberle, Rudolf, Chicago and London: University of Chicago Press.

Tönnies, F. (2001) *Community and Civil Society*, edited by Harris, J., Cambridge: Cambridge University Press.

United Nations Framework Convention on Climate Change (2009) *Copenhagen Accord*, Copenhagen: United Nations.

Urry, J. (2000) *Sociology beyond Societies: Mobilities for the Twenty-first Century,* London: Routledge.

Urry, J. (2005) 'The Complexities of the Global', *Theory, Culture & Society,* 22(5), pp. 235–54.

Urry, J. (2007) *Mobilities,* Cambridge: Polity Press.

Verity, F.E. (2005) *Insurance and Risk Management: Unravelling Civil Society?*, Adelaide: Flinders University.

Verity, F.E. (2006) 'Line dancing...not lion dancing!', *Australian Journal on Volunteering,* 11(1), pp. 50–58.

Verity, F., Jones, M., and Johnston, F. (2007) *The Doors are Open! Grenville Seniors Community Connections Hub*, Adelaide: Australian Centre for Community Services Research.

Verity, F. (2009) *Risk Management and Insurance*, unpublished report, Adelaide: Flinders University.

Verity, F.E. (2012) 'Risk Management – In the Insurance Market's Slipstream', in *Deliberations in Community Development: Balancing on the Edge*, edited by Rothe, J.P., Carroll, L.J. and Ozegovic, D., New York: Nova Science Publishers.

Walklate, S. and Mythen, G. (2010) 'Agency, reflexivity and risk: cosmopolitan, neurotic or predential citizen?', *The British Journal of Sociology*, 61(1), pp. 45–61.

Weber, M. (1947) *The Theory of Social and Economic Organisations*, New York: Oxford University Press.

Weber, M. (1964) *Economy and Society: An Outline of Interpretative Sociology*, New York: Free Press.

Weber, M. (1976 [1905]) *The Protestant Ethic and the Spirit of Capitalism,* London: Allen & Unwin.

West, B. (2008) 'Collective Memory and Crisis: 2002 Bali Bombings, National Archetypes and the Counter Narratives of Cosmopolitan Nationalism' *Sociology*, 44(4), pp. 337–53.

West, B. (2013) 'Rethinking Humanitarianism and the Nation: How Australian National Identity Facilitated the Charitable Response to the 2004 South

Asian Tsunami' *Working Paper* No. 04–13, Bristol University (accessed at http://www.bristol.ac.uk/spais/news/2013/233.html).

Williams, F., Bornat, J., Pereira, C. and Pilgrim, D. (eds) (1992) *Community Care: A Reader*, London: Macmillan.

William, F. (1999) 'Good enough principles for welfare', *Journal of Social Policy*, 28(4), pp. 667–87.

Willis, E. (1993) *The Sociological Quest,* St Leonards, NSW: Allen & Unwin.

Willis, E. (1999) *The Sociological Quest,* St Leonards, NSW: Allen & Unwin.

Wilson, J. (2000) 'Approaches to Supervision in Fieldwork' in *Fieldwork in the Human Services: Theory and Practice for Field Educators, Practice Teachers and Supervisors*, edited by Cooper, L., St Leonards: Allen & Unwin.

Women's International League for Peace and Freedom. (1985) *Years for Peace and Freedom*, London: WILPF.

World Health Organization. (2000) *Climate Change and Human Health: Impact and Adaption*, Geneva: WHO.

Yeung, K.S.S., Ho, A.P.Y., Lo, M.C.H. and Chan, E.A. (2010) 'Social Work Ethical Decision Making in an Inter-Disciplinary Context', *British Journal of Social Work,* 40(5), pp. 1573–90.

Young, I. (2000) *Inclusion and Democracy*, Oxford: Oxford University Press.

Zimbardo, P., and Boyd, J. (2008) *The Time Paradox: The New Psychology of Time that will Change your Life*, New York: Free Press.

Index